Lektürehilfen

Tennessee Williams

A Streetcar Named Desire

von Horst Mühlmann

Inhaltsangabe der Lektüre als mp3-Download unter www.klett.de/lernhilfen

Geben Sie den Online-Link 923000-0000 in das Suchfeld links oben ein.

Klett Lerntraining

Dr. Horst Mühlmann, Gymnasiallehrer für Englisch und Deutsch in Bonn, in der Lehrerfortbildung tätig.

Die Seiten- und Zeilenangaben zum Dramentext beziehen sich auf die Ausgabe: Tennessee Williams, *A Streetcar Named Desire*, with an introduction and annotations by Horst Mühlmann, Stuttgart: Ernst Klett Sprachen, 2008. ISBN 978-3-12-578211-2. Dieser Text folgt der Ausgabe: Tennessee Williams, *Plays 1937–1955*, ed. by Mel Gussow and Kenneth Holdich, New York: The Library of America, 2000, pp. 467–564.

Bibliografische Information der Deutschen Bibliothek
Die Deutsche Bibliothek verzeichnet diese Publikation in der Deutschen Nationalbibliografie; detaillierte bibliografische Daten sind im Internet über http://dnb.ddb.de abrufbar

Auflage 5. 4. 3. 2. | 2013 2012 2011 2010
Die letzten Zahlen bezeichnen jeweils die Auflage und das Jahr des Druckes.

http://www.klett.de/lernhilfen
Umschlagfoto: ullstein bild, Berlin
Satz: DOPPELPUNKT Auch & Grätzbach GbR, Stuttgart
Druck: Beltz Druckpartner GmbH & Co. KG, Hemsbach
Printed in Germany
ISBN 978-3-12-923045-9

9 783129 230459

Contents

Preface

Tennessee Williams' play *A Streetcar Named Desire* written from 1945 to 1947 was his second great success after *The Glass Menagerie* (1945) and established his fame as one of the greatest American playwrights. Some critics and the audience, however, first had some difficulties in understanding the dramatist's intention to convey an honest picture of human behaviour because *A Streetcar Named Desire* confronted them with themes such as sexual desire and violence, moral decay and insanity which in those days were not dealt with too openly on the stage. But Tennessee Williams won the Drama Critics Circle Award and the Pulitzer Prize, the greatest honour an American writer can achieve. Most of the critics realized Tennessee Williams' honest dramatic presentation of characters who challenge the spectators to reflect on the ambiguity of human nature, on loneliness and the lack of comprehension and compassion. As it is a modern tragedy the dramatist makes use of various stage effects to underline the characters' thoughts and emotions and to intensify the impact of the play on the audience. There have been many revivals of the play in many countries until today.
In order to understand the play, it is helpful to know something about the playwright's life, time and works since he frequently stated that he could only write about his own experiences and emotions transmuted into plays. In the following chapters of this study aid you are informed about the contents and the characters and offered an analysis and interpretation of the play. Tennessee Williams' view of *A Streetcar Named Desire* and its characters, his remarks about his work and his way of writing, the stage director's interpretation, reviews and extracts from various sources contribute to a better understanding of the play and offer ideas for your own interpretation. This also applies to the materials about the film version and its analysis. Finally, the impulses and model tasks could challenge you to work on various topics and problems and also inspire you to write creative texts about the play.

I The Author's Life, Time and Works

1. Tennessee Williams' Life and Works

Tennessee Williams, whose real name is Thomas Lanier Williams, was born on 26 March 1911 in Columbus, Mississippi. In 1938 he officially changed his name to Tennessee Williams. In his *Memoirs* (p. 12) he justifies his pen name by referring to the family tree. His father for instance directly descended from Tennessee's first senator and other illustrious ancestors in Tennessee. His father, Cornelius Coffin Williams, who worked for a telephone company as a regional manager, and then became a travelling salesman for a shoe company, was a heavy drinker, gambler and womanizer and usually away from home on business. But he was also totally honest and truth loving (cf. *Memoirs*, p. 13), which Tennessee gratefully stresses as his own trait of character he inherited from his father "both as writer and man" (cf. *Memoirs*, p. 243). His mother, Edwina Estelle Williams, was the daughter of the local Episcopal rector Walter Dakin, in whose rectory Tennessee lived together with his mother, his sister Rose and his grandparents. In his *Memoirs* (p. 11) Tennessee Williams describes that time as follows:

> "My first eight years of childhood in Mississippi were the most joyously innocent of my life, due to the beneficent homelife provided by my beloved Dakin grandparents, with whom we lived. And to the wild and sweet half-imaginary world in which my sister and our beautiful black nurse Ozzie existed, separate, almost invisible to anyone but our cabalistic circle of three."

Tennessee Williams and his sister could not forget Ozzie as long as they lived and were never prejudiced against black people. In his *Memoirs* (p. 252) Tennessee Williams describes his visit to New York with his sister at Christmas 1975: "Rose is fond of the blacks, as I am, perhaps because of our devotion to our beautiful black nurse Ozzie when we were children in Mississippi. She always used to conclude her letters to me with, 'Love to my children, white and black.' I noticed that in New York, on the streets and in stores, Rose was continually waving to children of both races."

When he was a boy, Tennessee Williams liked to listen to animal stories told by Ozzie and to the stories from Dickens and Shakespeare his mother read to him when he suffered from diphtheria and Bright's disease and was unable to walk for a year and a half.

> "Prior to it, I had been a little boy with a robust, aggressive, almost bullying nature. During the illness, I learned to play, alone, games of my own invention. [...] I had already read *The Iliad* and I turned the black and red cards into two opposite armies battling for Troy." (*Memoirs*, p. 11)

But during his long sickness he became shy and effeminate, also because of his overprotective mother who did not like him to play with boys. His sensitivity and shyness caused his father to believe that he was a "sissy" and he called him "Miss Nancy".
The "charmed time" in Columbus ended in 1918 when his father became a manager in a shoe factory in St. Louis and the family left Mississippi. In his *Memoirs* (p. 14) Tennessee writes:

> "The malign exercise of snobbery in 'middle American' life was an utterly new experience to Rose and to me and I think its sudden and harsh discovery had a traumatic effect on our lives. It had never occurred to us that material disadvantages could cut us off from friends. It was about this time, age eleven or twelve, that I started writing stories – it was a compensation, perhaps ..."

Tennessee Williams became introverted and felt lonely except when he was together with his sister and his grandfather. At school he was ostracized and taunted and thus felt isolated except for his close relationship to his beloved sister Rose. After the elementary school he attended the Junior High School in St. Louis and began writing on a second-hand typewriter given to him by his mother. His short story *Isolated* was printed in the school newspaper and his poem "Demon Smoke" in the school yearbook. During that time tension increased between his parents, his father's drinking problems became chronic, his sister was increasingly mentally disturbed and his mother suffered from hysteria – motifs he made use of in his works. In a talk with Studs Terkel in 1961 Tennessee Williams states: "Two different couples, my grandparents who grew together in wholeness and love, and my parents who split violently apart and tore the children apart through division and conflict. Those are the two backgrounds that I had as a forming person." (*Conversations*, p. 87)
In 1926 Tennessee Williams entered University City High School in St. Louis and in his *Memoirs* he writes that his "adolescent problems took their most violent form on a shyness of a pathological degree" (p. 17) and in his last year at school he describes his behaviour as follows: "It was still almost entirely impossible for me to speak aloud in classroom. And, teachers stopped asking me questions because when they did, I would produce a voice that was hardly intelligible, my throat would be so tight with panic." (p. 23)
In 1927 he won his first prizes for an essay and a film review and in 1928 he published a short story in *Weird Tales* magazine. In the same year he travelled to Europe with his grandfather and visited France, Italy, Switzerland, Germany, the Netherlands and England, which he frequently did during his life. In his *Memoirs* (cf. pp. 22 f) he describes a "miracle" he experienced in Co-

logne Cathedral which he could not forget. As he suffered from a phobia, he felt a mystic hand upon his head and the phobia disappeared. "I have never doubted the existence of God nor have I ever neglected to kneel in prayer when a situation in which I found myself (and there have been many) seemed critical enough in my opinion to merit the Lord's attention and, I trust, intervention."

After graduating from high school in 1929 he entered the University of Missouri at Columbia during the great American depression intending to study journalism but concentrated more on playwriting in his third and last year at the university. In 1931 his father insisted on his leaving the university because he had failed Reserve Officers' Training Corps (ROTC) and also because of his family's financial difficulties. Instead, he had to work hard as a clerk in the shoe company that employed his father, which he describes as follows:

> "The two years I spent in that corporation were indescribable torment to me as an individual but of immense value to me as a writer for they gave me first-hand knowledge of what it means to be a small wage earner in a hopelessly routine job. I had been writing since childhood and I continued writing while I was employed by the shoe company. When I came home from work I would tank up on black coffee so I could remain awake most of the night, writing short stories which I could not sell. Gradually my health broke down. One day, coming home from work, I collapsed and was removed to hospital." (*Essays*, p. 60)

In his *Memoirs* (p. 37) Tennessee Williams writes: "I started writing at night. I would write and complete one story a week and mail it, as soon as I finished, to the distinguished story magazine called *Story*. [...] At first the editors encouraged me with little personal notes of criticism. But soon I began to receive those dreadful 'form' rejections."

After his recovery Tennessee Williams moved to Memphis and stayed there with his beloved grandparents, who enabled him to continue his studies at Washington University in St. Louis in 1935 and at the State University of Iowa where he studied playwriting. During that time he continuously wrote plays. In his *Memoirs* (p. 40) he writes: "My first play was produced when I was 24 years old and staying in my grandparents' home in Memphis the summer of 1934. This play (*Cairo, Shanghai, Bombay!*) was successfully produced by The Rose Arbor Players, a little-theater group, in Memphis." Two other of his first plays were produced by a semi-professional group called The Mummers of St. Louis.

Tennessee Williams also published poetry in the university magazine and mainly read the works of modern European dramatists such as Anton Chekhov, August Strindberg and Henrik Ibsen. The strongest influence on his work he attributes to Chekhov, whose play *The Sea Gull* he considered "the greatest of modern plays, with the possible exception of Brecht's *Mother*

The French Quarter in New Orleans

Courage" (*Memoirs*, p. 41). He also underlines the influence of D. H. Lawrence on his work, in particular the novel *Lady Chatterley's Lover* and its liberation from the restrictions of traditional ideas about social and sexual behaviour. As he also wrote numerous poems, his favourite American poet was Hart Crane (1899–1932), whom he valued above other poets "because of his organic purity and sheer breathless power" (*Essays*, p. 6) and from whose poem "The Broken Tower" the playwright quotes four lines as the epigraph for *A Streetcar Named Desire*. Moreover, they both experienced a partly unhappy childhood and were homosexual. Before Tennessee Williams became aware of his homosexuality, Hazel, a fourteen-year-old girl, was his only great love when he was sixteen but she only allowed him to kiss her twice a year and refused to marry him several years later (cf. *Memoirs*, pp. 15 ff).
After taking a degree in English at the State University of Iowa in 1938 he went to different places in the United States and earned his living by taking odd jobs such as the job of a liftboy, waiter, teletype operator, cashier, movie usher and farm-hand. All the while he kept on writing plays. In December 1938 he stayed in the French Quarter of New Orleans for the first time of many stays there. According to his brother Dakin, he went there "with no job, no money, and no real prospect of making any. Tennessee took a bus to New Orleans. He wanted to get away from St. Louis and his family, to write and to live for as close to nothing as possible. And, no doubt, he also wanted privacy, because it was in New Orleans that he 'came out', the gay way of saying that he had decided on his way of sex and no longer wanted to suppress it. [...] He said he was fascinated by the city, which was true. He did love New Orleans; he has always said it is his favorite city in America, perhaps in the world. He walked the city for miles, explored every stone of the Vieux Carré, the old French quarter where he lived [...]." (Dakin Williams / Shepherd Mead, *Tennessee Williams. An Intimate Biography*, p. 73; in the following text quoted Dakin Williams)
In the following years Williams also went to various places such as California, New York, St. Louis, Key West and was always writing plays. As he was often short of money, he lived on the money sent to him by his grandmother and the money he earned for several odd jobs. In an essay of 1957 he even writes: "I lived on stolen eggs and avocados and dried peas for a week, and also on a faint hope stirred by a letter from a lady in New York whose name was Audrey Wood" (*Essays*, p. 86). She was head of the best theatrical agency and began to represent him in 1939. As she succeeded in obtaining for him a Rockefeller Fellowship or grant of 1,000 dollars, which were passed out to gifted young writers, he could live on the money and continue writing and rewriting plays. At her instigation he went to Hollywood in 1943 to write screenplays for MGM (Metro-Goldwyn-Mayer) but without being successful.
Though his father was against it, his mother allowed a brain operation (prefrontal lobotomy) of his beloved sister Rose in 1943 because she had been

diagnosed schizophrenia since 1937. As the operation failed (it has no longer been practised since then) and destroyed her memory, his sister became paranoid. Tennessee Williams lived in New York and was informed by a letter without being able to prevent the operation. Throughout his life he took good care of Rose and visited her frequently. He arranged her being taken care of in several sanatoriums and nursing homes and also bought a house for her in Key West so that she could live near him.

Before writing *A Streetcar Named Desire* Tennessee Williams rewrote the dramatic adaptation of his short story *Portrait of a Girl in Glass*, called *The Gentleman Caller*, with the new title *The Glass Menagerie*, which was produced in Chicago in 1944, received excellent reviews and ran for more than three months. The protagonist Laura, a sensitive and fragile girl, was modelled after his beloved sister Rose and Laura's mother after his own mother. The performance of the play on Broadway in 1945 was sold out three months before it opened. It was Tennessee Williams' first great success and won the New York Drama Critics Circle Award. Tennessee Williams had become famous overnight and was able to overcome his financial difficulties due to his income from the stage production.

After the operation of his eye cataract he went to Mexico where he worked on the play *The Moth*, then called *Blanche's Chair in the Moon* and renamed *The Primary Colors* and then *The Poker Night*, which he finished in Key West, Florida in 1947 with the final title *A Streetcar Named Desire*. The playwright stated that the character of Blanche was partly modelled after his beloved sister Rose:

> "I believe I was thinking of my sister because she was madly in love with some young man at the International Shoe Company who paid her court. He was extremely handsome, and she was profoundly in love with him. Whenever the phone would ring, she'd nearly faint. She'd think it was he calling for a date, you know? They saw each other every other night, and then one time he just didn't call anymore. That was when Rose first began to go into a mental decline. From that vision *Streetcar* evolved. I called it at the time, *Blanche's Chair in the Moon,* which is a very bad title. But it was from that image, you know, of a woman sitting by a window that *Streetcar* came to me." (*Conversations*, pp. 330 f)

But Blanche also seems to have some traits of Tennessee Williams whose moral code was "Nothing human disgusts me unless it's unkind, violent" (Dakin Williams, p. 237). This is also expressed by Blanche: "Deliberate cruelty is not forgivable. It is the one unforgivable thing in my opinion and it is the one thing of which I have never, never been guilty." (*Streetcar*, p. 96, ll. 24–26) In his *Memoirs* (p. 170) the playwright stresses this idea: "I have never blamed anyone for anything but deliberate cruelty, for there has always been in me the conviction of Blanche, that 'deliberate cruelty is the one unforgivable thing'." Moreover, he underlines like Blanche that he has "always depended on the kindness of strangers" (*Streetcar*, p. 107, l. 36; cf. *Memoirs*, p. 131).

A Streetcar Named Desire starring Jessica Tandy as Blanche, Marlon Brando as Stanley, Kim Hunter as Stella and Karl Malden as Mitch was produced by Irene Selznick and directed by Elia Kazan in cooperation with Tennessee Williams. But Williams thought that it was "a certain failure" when he saw the first rehearsals. In his *Memoirs* (p. 134) he writes: "I was once again certain that I was a dying artist and not even the least bit sure that I was an artist." Before the New York opening of the play it was performed in New Haven in early November 1947 without great public interest. But the performances in Boston and Philadelphia were increasingly successful. The New York opening on 3 December 1947 was a tremendous success and ran for 855 performances. Tennessee Williams won the Drama Critics Circle Award, the Donaldson Award and the Pulitzer Prize, the greatest honour an American writer can achieve. He became an internationally recognized dramatist and also a wealthy man due to his income from the stage productions as well as the selling of the screen rights.

In 1948 his parents separated and Tennessee Williams travelled extensively in Europe and the USA and also went to Mexico, Hong Kong, Thailand, Japan and other countries for holidays or to see various rehearsals and performances of his plays for instance in London, Paris, Rome, Hamburg, Stockholm. He stated: "I'm restless. I like traveling." (*Conversations*, p. 340) In London he met Laurence Olivier, the director of *A Streetcar Named Desire*, and his wife Vivien Leigh playing the role of Blanche, which she also did in Elia Kazan's successful cinematic adaptation of the play together with Marlon Brando in 1951.

The reviews of the London performance were predominantly positive but some critics condemned the play and wrote for instance that it was "a squalid anecdote of a nymphomaniac's decay in a New Orleans slum", despite the cuts such as the reference to homosexuality demanded by the Lord Chamberlain. Though in Parliament the misuse of public funds for immoral plays was disputed, the play ran for 326 performances. In Paris the reviews were less favourable. Critics for instance described the play as "filled with undressing, morbid events, fights and games [...] obscenities and murders." But Jean Cocteau's version of the play ran for 233 performances (cf. Sambrook, pp. 83 f).

When Rome became "the city of his dreams" (Dakin Williams, p. 153), Tennessee Williams wrote his short novel *The Roman Spring of Mrs. Stone* (1950) about the fading beauty of an American actress and her sexual affair with an Italian gigolo. Some critics believe it to be "really a self-portrait of Tennessee" (Dakin Williams, p. 154) since "it was not unusual for him to transfer his own feelings to those of a female character" (Dakin Williams, p. 47).

Tennessee Williams also met numerous famous writers such as Carson McCullers, Thornton Wilder, Truman Capote, Noel Coward, Jean Cocteau and Henry Faulkner. In 1959 he went to Havana where he met Ernest Hemingway

and through him Fidel Castro, an admirer of his work. Finally he settled down in Key West, Florida, where he had finished *A Streetcar Named Desire* and where he could work best as he believed.
When he was asked in an interview in 1965 which of his plays were his favourite plays, he answered: "The plays of mine which I think had more importance were *Streetcar, The Glass Menagerie* – the two most people think are my best – and *Cat on a Hot Tin Roof*." (*Conversations*, p. 117)
The cinematic adaptations of *The Glass Menagerie* (1950), *A Streetcar Named Desire* (1951), *The Rose Tattoo* (1955) and *Cat on a Hot Tin Roof* (1958) were the most successful films whereas the other eleven films based on plays by Tennessee Williams were not very much appreciated by critics and the audience or were more or less considered failures. Also his short novel *The Roman Spring of Mrs. Stone* (1950) was turned into a film starring his favourite actress Vivien Leigh. The film *Baby Doll* (1956) about a triangle relationship between a childlike bride, her wealthy fiancé and his enemy, for which Tennessee Williams wrote the script, was condemned by the Catholic Legion of Decency and was no commercial success. Whether successful or not, the roles in the films beginning with *A Streetcar Named Desire* until the film *The Milk Train does not Stop Here Any More* (1962) were played by some of the best actors of his time such as Vivien Leigh, Marlon Brando, Karl Malden, Elizabeth Taylor, Ava Gardner, Deborah Kerr, Katherine Hepburn, Richard Burton, Anna Magnani, Burt Lancaster, Paul Newman, Jane Fonda.
Tennessee Williams was mainly interested in his work and wanted to deal with essentially human problems that are supposed to concern everybody. He did not want to write "political plays" but he spoke out against the nuclear blasts at Hiroshima and Nagasaki and the Korean and Vietnam wars. He called the atom bomb a toy "from the Devil's workshop, a toy that may eventually extinguish all intelligent life" (*Essays*, p. 170). In 1966 he issued a public statement against the American involvement in Vietnam and in 1971 he spoke out against the Vietnam War at a rally in New York. In an interview of 1967 he states: "The way they [the American army] burn people alive [by Napalm] and the way they spray chemicals over the rice fields so they will starve; I don't need to list the instruments [...] they are incredibly cruel and, believe me, nothing that will be won out of this war will be worth the life of a single man who died in it, in my opinion." (*Conversations*, p. 128) He also strongly opposed the McCarthy hearings which he called a "witch hunt" for communists and an example of America's moral decay. Referring to the Vietnam War he said: "We're the death merchants of the world, this once great and beautiful democracy. People think I'm a communist [for saying this], but I hate all bureaucracy, all isms. I'm a revolutionary only in the sense that I want to see us escape from this sort of trap." (*Conversations*, p. 292)
He underlined that racial discrimination in the USA was intolerable and supported the Civil Rights Movement:

> "I am terribly involved in the Black movement because I think it is the most horrible thing (racism). I think that the white people in America, southern and northern equally – even more northern – have exercised the most dreadful injustices, historically, and even now [1974], discrimination, and not just in terms of jobs." (*Conversations*, p. 267)

He was "an intensely patriotic American" but in his interview with Studs Terkel in 1961 he also said: "I'm afraid of thinking that all the rest of the world is in error and we're [the Americans are] totally right. Nobody is right. And the whole meaning of all my work is that there is no such thing as complete right and complete wrong, complete black, complete white." (*Conversations*, p. 90) Tennessee Williams was a heavy smoker and had already become increasingly dependent on alcohol and drugs since 1949. He was afraid of having lung cancer, frequently suffered from depression, underwent psychotherapy, was diagnosed paranoid symptoms, was sometimes confused and disoriented but recovered sufficiently after being taken to a hospital in St. Louis by his brother Dakin because of a physical and mental breakdown and medically treated there in 1969. In the same year his brother urged him to convert from the Episcopalian belief to Catholicism but in an interview of 1970 Tennessee Williams states: "My real religion is my writing. I didn't go to church before my conversion, and I don't go now that I'm officially Catholic. When I'm scared, I do pray a lot, though, and I do believe there is a God." (*Conversations*, p. 150)

Tennessee Williams lived together with Frank Merlo for sixteen years until his partner, who used to smoke four packs of cigarettes a day, was diagnosed lung cancer and died in 1963. Though Merlo's death caused a deep depression and heavy dependence on drugs, he tirelessly went on writing, rewriting and altering plays and seeing and criticizing the stage productions and cinematic adaptations of his plays.

Frequently he visited previews and revivals of his most successful plays in the USA and Europe. But after 1962 none of his rather experimental and innovative new plays was really successful since neither the critics nor the audience could understand or appreciate them, for instance the play *Vieux Carré* (1977) about the education of the artist in loneliness and despair and whose title reminds of the setting of *A Streetcar Named Desire*. Another of his unsuccessful plays was *A Lovely Sunday for Creve Coeur* (1978) about loneliness and the need for understanding. In an article that appeared in *The New York Times* (May 8, 1977) he stated: "I am widely regarded as the ghost of a writer, a ghost still visible, excessively solid of flesh and perhaps too ambulatory, but a writer remembered mostly for works which were staged between 1944 and 1961."

As *A Streetcar Named Desire* is regarded as an American classic, there have been many revivals of the play, TV presentations and other adaptations in the United States, in Europe and other parts of the world.

In December 1982 Tennessee Williams was hospitalized in Key West suffering from drug toxicity. He died lonely in New York on 24 February 1983 at the Elysée Hotel choking to death on a barbiturate-bottle cap.

Tennessee Williams was an extraordinarily productive writer and wrote more than 70 plays, about 40 of them short plays. About 100 short stories and three collections of poems were published. He wrote two novels, screenplays, essays, his *Memoirs*, ballads, songs and a libretto. Moreover, he wrote a large number of letters and gave many interviews.

In his *Memoirs* (p. 85) Tennessee Williams states that "what is in these memoirs is mostly the barest periphery of that which is my intense life, for my intense life is my work." Wherever he was, he was continuously writing and rewriting his works. Apart from the plays *The Glass Menagerie* and *A Streetcar Named Desire* his most successful plays were *The Rose Tattoo* (1951) about the joys and discontents of sex, for which he received the Tony Award for best play, *Cat on a Hot Tin Roof* (1955) about the moral decay of a Southern family, for which he again won the Drama Critics Circle Award and the Pulitzer Prize, *Sweet Bird of Youth* (1956) about desire and love, *Orpheus Descending* (1957) about the failure of love in an intolerant Southern province, and *The Night of the Iguana* (1962) about human loneliness, which won his fourth Drama Critics Circle Award as best play though Tennessee Williams disliked the stage production since contrary to the published version it did not truly express his intention.

Apart from winning the Drama Critics Circle Award four times and the Pulitzer Prize twice, Tennessee Williams was frequently honoured. In 1962 for instance he became lifetime member of the American Academy of Arts and Letters and received the National Institute of Arts and Letters Gold Medal for Drama seven years later. He got honorary doctorates from the University of Columbia, the Purdue University and Harvard University. He was invited by President John F. Kennedy to a banquet at the White House. In 1979 President Jimmy Carter presented him with the Presidential Medal of Freedom, the highest award a civilian can be given by the Administration. He was appointed Distinguished Writer in Residence at the University of British Columbia in Vancouver in 1980, received the Common Wealth Award together with Harold Pinter in 1981 and New York's city medallion of honour a year before his death.

In 1989 Tennessee Williams was honoured by a brass star featuring his name and a bronze plaque set into the pavements of the University City Loop in St. Louis, the city's Walk of Fame, which advances "the knowledge, awareness and appreciation of great St. Louisans and their accomplishments" (cf. http://www.stlouiswalkoffame.org.html). The plaque contains the following brief biography:

> "One of the greatest twentieth century playwrights, Tennessee Williams attended Soldan high school, University City high school and Washington University, before graduating from the University of Iowa. His plays explore what he called 'the unlighted sides' of human nature with great insight. He won Pulitzer Prizes for *Streetcar Named Desire* and *Cat On A Hot Tin Roof*. Those works, along with *Glass Menagerie* and *Night of the Iguana*, also won New York Drama Critics Circle Awards. Williams wrote nearly thirty full-length plays, two novels, and a number of short stories and plays."

It might be interesting that among the numerous other St. Louis Walk of Fame honourees are Joseph Pulitzer (founder of the Pulitzer Prize), T. S. Eliot (winner of the Nobel Prize for Literature in 1948), Kate Chopin (short story writer), Grace Bumbry (mezzo soprano), Tina Turner (pop and rock singer), Miles Davis (jazz musician), Scott Joplin (ragtime composer and musician), Albert King (blues guitarist), Jimmy Connors (tennis champion), Ozzie Smith (baseball player), etc.
New Orleans celebrates Tennessee Williams' birthday annually in late March. The programme includes panel discussions, theatrical performances, a one-act play competition, lectures, literary walking tours, musical performances, and a book fair (cf. http://www.tennesseewilliams.net/index.php?topic/html).

2. New Orleans and *A Streetcar Named Desire*

In an interview of 1957 Tennessee Williams said: "New Orleans is my favorite city of America [...] of all the world, actually." (*Conversations*, p. 48)
In 1938 he went to New Orleans the first time and stayed in its oldest part, the French Quarter or Vieux Carré, which became the setting of *A Streetcar Named Desire* and the title of his play *Vieux Carré* (1977). The title of the play *A Streetcar Named Desire* refers to the tram line to Desire Street and is used by the playwright symbolically to allude to one of the main topics of the play. In a letter of January 15, 1946 to his agent Audrey Wood the dramatist writes:

> "Right now I am doing more with the sisters [Blanche and Stella], it is now set in New Orleans and is called 'A Street-car Named Desire' – there is one by that title that runs close by my apartment, and proceeding in the other direction down the next street is one called 'Cemeteries'. In spite of this I am not really in a very morbid state of mind, as this might suggest." (*Letters*, p. 36)

In 1948 the tram was replaced by a bus. The original streetcar "Desire" of 1906 is shown in the Mardi Gras and Jazz Museum in New Orleans. But also the Pennsylvania Trolley Museum in Washington, Pennsylvania claims that they have the restored original tram.

New Orleans, located on the banks of the Mississippi River to a large extent below sea level, is one of the oldest towns in the USA and was founded in 1718 by the French Mississippi Company and called La Nouvelle-Orléans after the Duke of Orléans, Philippe II of France. It is the largest city in Louisiana, a French colony until 1763 when it was ceded to the Spanish Empire, reverted to French control in 1801 and sold to the United States by Napoleon two years later. When the southern US states (the Confederate states) decided to secede from the northern US states (the Union) and maintain slavery, the Civil War (1861–65) was fought and finally won by the northern states. In 1961 Abraham Lincoln, the 16th president of the United States, had issued a proclamation freeing all slaves, which also contributed to the economic decline of the plantation owners.

New Orleans grew rapidly and has become one of the major ports in the United States because of its ideal position at the mouth of the Mississippi. But as large parts of New Orleans are situated below sea level or barely above sea level, the city has always been vulnerable to flooding either by the Mississippi or the frequent tornados and major hurricanes. Though floodwalls, the so-called levees, have been constructed, 80% of the city was flooded when Hurricane Katrina devastated the city on 29 August 2005 and most of its residents had to be evacuated. The French Quarter which lies above sea level was not destroyed but the city's reconstruction and repopulation took a long time.

In *A Streetcar Named Desire* Tennessee Williams does not mention that New Orleans has always been threatened by hurricanes. He concentrates on such aspects as music and night life and their psychological impact on the characters of his play. He rarely refers to historical events but mentions the Napoleonic Code to stress Stanley's attitude towards money and his friendship to Mitch, who was in the same army corps. When Mitch asks Blanche: "All quiet on the Potomac?" (*Streetcar,* p. 45, l. 35), the dramatist ironically refers to the Potomac River where numerous battles of the American Civil War were fought. He also stresses Stanley's pride in having survived the landing at Salerno in the Second World War, which taught him "to hold front position in this rat-race [of life]" (*Streetcar*, p. 19, ll. 12 f; p. 26, l. 34; p. 77, ll. 34 f; p. 100, ll. 16 ff).

The architecture in New Orleans and its cultural life reflect the city's multicultural heritage. The house Tennessee Williams chooses as the setting of *A Streetcar Named Desire* reminds of the Creole two-storey townhouses with iron balconies in the French Quarter. The characters of his play represent the city's population of different ethnicity and nationality such as Franco-Americans, Creoles, African-Americans, Hispanics, Latinos, immigrants from Europe and Asians to convey an authentic multicultural background. Due to its multilingual heritage he also uses some Creole, French and Spanish words and sentences. He refers to the humid subtropical climate, the port, some streets, the Lake Pontchartrain in the north of New Orleans and the Cathedral. He also makes use of the city's musical heritage of jazz and blues and mentions Mardi Gras (the carnival the day before Ash Wednesday), Western Comfort (the city's brand of whisky), the long nightlife, gambling and also crime in the French Quarter to convey its "raffish charm" and atmosphere of *joie de vivre* and moral decay.

But the dramatist does not use such elements only to give an authentic picture of New Orleans but frequently makes use of them in a dramatic and symbolical way. Thus the noise of the L&N locomotive for instance allows Stanley to overhear Blanche without being noticed by her. When she arrives at a street called Elysian Fields after having taken the streetcar named Desire and transferred to one called Cemeteries, Tennessee Williams already alludes to Blanche's fate at the beginning of the play. The dramatic and stylistic devices used by the author will be dealt with more closely in Chapter III of this study guide.

Tennessee Williams' characters also represent the change from the Old Southern way of life of the cotton plantation owners, whose wealth was mainly based on slavery, to the new way of American life. Blanche for instance represents the decaying culture and moral decline of the old Southerners but also

Southern values of beauty, elegance and education whereas Stanley seems to stand for the New South and the modern America of industrialization and materialism but also of hard work and determination. In an essay that appeared in the *New York Times,* August 13, 1950 Williams writes: "Now there are only two cities left in America with a romantic appeal, however vestigial, and they are, of course, New Orleans and San Francisco. Our industrial dynamism has dispelled whatever magic the other great cities may once have possessed." (*Essays*, p. 30) As his "scenes of degradation" in his play *Baby Doll* infuriated Southerners in 1957, the playwright said in an interview:

> "I write out of love for the South. But I can't expect Southerners to realize that my writing about them is an expression of love. It is out of a regret for a South that no longer exists that I write of the forces that have destroyed it. I don't write about the North, because I feel nothing for it but eagerness to get out of it. I don't write about the North because – so far as I know – they never had anything to lose, culturally. But the South once had a way of life that I am just old enough to remember – a culture that had grace, elegance ... an inbred culture ... not a society based on money, as in the North. I write out of regret for that." (*Conversations*, p. 43)

II *A Streetcar Named Desire*

www.klett.de

1. Contents and Commentary

Scene One

Before the dialogue of the play begins Tennessee Williams describes the setting of the play and the situation presented at the beginning of the first scene in rather long and detailed stage directions. He thus conveys background information about New Orleans and the multiracial life in the French Quarter to the reader and the stage director who is supposed to make use of it for the stage production.
The first scene starts in front of a typical house in the French Quarter with two storeys, outside stairs and galleries. It is situated on the corner of Elysian Fields Avenue, a street between the Mississippi and the rails of the Louisville and Nashville line. Though it is a poor section of the town with shabby wooden houses, the dramatist stresses its crude charm.
The action begins at dusk early in May when the turquoise colour of the sky softens "the atmosphere of decay". It is still warm and the air is filled with the smell of bananas and coffee from the warehouses of the port. One can hear the music of black entertainers at a barroom and in particular of "a tinny piano", the dramatist calls the "Blue Piano" which "expresses the spirit of life" in the French Quarter.
The rather uncomplicated multiracial and multicultural life in the French Quarter is also underlined when the playwright describes New Orleans as a "cosmopolitan city where there is a relatively warm and easy intermingling of races". Moreover, the play begins with a talk of a white woman called Eunice, the landlady, who lives upstairs in the two-storey house, and a coloured woman, her neighbour. Their talk is accompanied by the music of the "Blue Piano" and the voices of the people on the street, for instance of a sailor and a tamale vendor. When the sailor asks the women where a certain bar is, the coloured woman warns him of that rip-off place.
Stanley Kowalski and his friend Mitch, both in their late twenties, appear. They wear work clothes and obviously want to go to a bowling alley because Stanley carries his bowling jacket. They are talking about betting and leave after Stanley has thrown a blood-stained package of meat up to his wife Stella on the first floor landing. In a stage direction she is described as a twenty-five-year old gentle woman with "a background obviously quite different from her husband's". She follows her husband to watch him bowling.

While the coloured woman continues laughing about Stanley's behaviour, Blanche arrives with a travelling bag and is asked by Eunice if she could help her. After having taken the streetcar named Desire and then changed trams for Cemeteries, Blanche cannot believe that she has arrived at her sister's home since she is totally disappointed and shocked by the poor street called Elysian Fields and the run-down house. Contrary to the poor surroundings Blanche is dressed elegantly. Since Blanche is not willing to go and find her sister, the black woman leaves to fetch Stella and Eunice lets Blanche enter the small flat downstairs, which only consists of two untidy rooms and a bathroom. Eunice tells Blanche that Stella had already talked about her and asks several questions about her, which Blanche first answers but then tells that she feels tired. But the reader (or the theatregoer) learns that Blanche lived on a plantation in Mississippi and was a teacher. Eunice feels offended by Blanche and leaves to tell Stella to hurry up. Blanche takes a whisky bottle out of a closet, quickly drinks half a tumbler of it, replaces the bottle and washes the tumbler out in order to hide her drinking alcohol.

When Stella arrives the sisters embrace each other joyfully but Blanche's behaviour is awkward since she talks a lot in a "feverish" way, asks Stella to turn off the bright light, contradicts herself when she describes the flat as "horrible" and as a "convenient location", first pretends that she does not know where the whisky is and then fetches the bottle to have a another drink but tells Stella that she is no drunkard. Nevertheless she pretends to be honest and asks her sister how she is able to live at such a primitive place. Stella replies that it is not as bad as Blanche believes since New Orleans is different from other cities.

Without being asked by her sister why she could stop teaching before the end of the term, Blanche tells Stella that the high school superintendent allowed her to leave for a while because of her nervous exhaustion. After talking about their figures, the narrow flat, the folding bed in the kitchen where Blanche is going to sleep, Blanche asks her sister about her husband Stanley and his friends. When she learns that he is Polish and rather uneducated, she fears that he might not like her. Stella tells her sister that she loves him and alludes to her sexual desire when she admits that she "can hardly stand it when he is away for a night".

Without being asked by her sister, Blanche reproachfully tells her that she stayed at the plantation Belle Reve whereas Stella left for New Orleans. Despite her efforts Belle Reve was lost after the death of their relatives Blanche had to care for as long as they were mortally ill. She reproaches Stella for leaving her alone and coming home only for the funerals. As the burden of caring for the dying members of her family fell on her alone, she finally insults Stella, who starts crying and leaves for the bathroom.

Stanley, Steve and Mitch appear in front of the house laughing about Steve's dirty joke. They arrange to meet to play poker the next day in Stanley's flat and not at Mitch's because his mother is sick. Eunice tells her husband Steve to come home at once. The three men part laughing and shouting. Stanley enters his flat where he meets Blanche whom he offers a shot of whisky, which she rejects telling the lie that she is not fond of drinking alcohol. Stanley seems to be suspicious about that when he recognizes that there is less whisky in the bottle than before. He takes off his sweaty shirt and asks her several questions about her job as a teacher, about how long she intends to stay with them and about her marriage. All his direct questions show that his wife has spoken about Blanche, who suddenly feels sick when she is reminded of her dead husband.

Scene Two

The following evening Blanche is taking a hot bath while Stella is dressing. They want to go to a restaurant and then to a show as long as Stanley and his friends are playing poker because Stella believes that her sister will not like it and is in a nervous condition after the loss of the plantation. That is why she asks Stanley to be nice to Blanche and not to tell anything about her pregnancy. Stanley, however, supposes that the plantation was sold and insists on seeing the bill of sale since he believes that they have the right to get a portion of the money and that according to the Napoleonic Code he owns what his wife owns and vice versa. Stella does not know what happened to Belle Reve and – contrary to her husband – does not believe that Blanche has swindled them. But Stanley pulls Blanche's dresses, furs and costume jewellery out of her trunk and believes that she has bought them for thousands of dollar. Though Stella tells him that he is mistaken when he thinks that it is real gold, he intends to have it checked by a jeweller.

When he is told by Stella to leave the room and let Blanche dress, he points out that he will not be commanded by his wife. Blanche dresses after having drawn the curtains between the two rooms. When she appears again, she seductively asks Stanley to button up the dress, let her have a drag on his cigarette and expects him to admire her. But Stanley does not really care about her wishes and her vanity and is therefore characterized by Blanche as open-minded and a bit primitive.

After Stella left to buy a coke-lemon for her sister, Blanche wants to stop the "double-talk" and answer Stanley's questions about the plantation. When Stanley wants to see the papers and against her wishes also takes her late husband's love-letters and poems and examines everything, Blanche nearly faints with exhaustion. He decides to have the papers studied by a lawyer and repeats that it is his right according to the Napoleonic Code, also because Stella is pregnant.

When Stella returns, Blanche embraces her and expresses that she is happy about her getting a baby. She also tells her that she has treated the loss of the plantation as a joke and even flirted with Stanley. Then Stanley's poker partners arrive and the two sisters leave for their night out.

Scene Three

When Stanley, Steve, Pablo and Mitch begin to play poker, Stanley dominates his friends. He pushes some watermelon rinds to the floor because he only wants to have cards, chips and whisky on a poker table. When Mitch mentions that he has to go home soon because his mother is sick, Stanley tells him to leave and ridicules him when Mitch goes to the bathroom. Stanley gets impatient when Steve tells a joke and he does not laugh like Steve and Pablo.

Before Stella and Blanche enter, Blanche asks her sister how she looks and powders her face. Stanley is rude to them because the women disturb him. When Blanche goes to the bathroom she meets Mitch, who seems to be impressed by her. As he behaves politely, Blanche asks her sister whether Mitch is married, what kind of job he has and if he will be promoted. Stella believes that only Stanley has a chance to get ahead. The sisters put some other clothes on and when they laugh about Eunice and Pablo's wife who are overweight, Stanley tells them to be quiet and turns the radio off when Blanche listens to rumba music. He orders Mitch to sit down when his friend wants to go to the toilet and ridicules him again.

Mitch leaves for the toilet and meets Blanche who asks him for a cigarette. When he opens his silver cigarette case, she tells him that the inscription on it is a line from her favourite sonnet by the English poet Elizabeth Barrett Browning. Mitch tells her that he got the case from a girl who knew that she was going to die and agrees with Blanche who tells him that sick people are full of sincere affection. She explains the meaning of her name and mentions that her ancestors were French Huguenots. But she also tells him lies, for instance that she does not drink much alcohol and that her sister is older than she is. She asks him to put a Chinese lantern over the light bulb without telling that she fears to be recognized as older than she pretends to be. She continues telling lies, e.g. that she visits her sister, who does not feel well, in order to help her and that she is a high school teacher for English without telling that she was dismissed. When she switches on the radio and begins to waltz, Mitch is delighted but Stanley appears and throws the radio out of the window. Stella asks the poker players to leave but Stanley, who is drunk, beats her while all the others are upset about it. Stanley's friends force him into the bedroom to calm him down.

Blanche and Stella hurry upstairs to spend the night with Eunice while Mitch, Pablo and Steve lead Stanley into the bathroom to sober up after a shower and then they go home. After a while Stanley comes out of the bathroom, begins to sob and wants Stella to come down again. Eunice does not answer

his phone call but blames him for his violent behaviour and shuts the door. When Stanley shouts for Stella at the pitch of his voice, she comes downstairs and Stanley carries her into the bedroom.
When Blanche comes downstairs to look for her sister, she meets Mitch who tells her that Stanley and Stella are crazy about each other. They sit down on the steps, smoke a cigarette and Blanche thanks him for being so kind to her.

Scene Four

The following morning Stella is lying on her bed whereas Blanche enters nervously after a sleepless night and hysterically asks her sister why she could return to Stanley and sleep with him. Stella excuses Stanley's behaviour as typical of him when he is drunk and tells her that he is ashamed of his behaviour last night but has always smashed things. He has left to have the radio repaired. Blanche cannot understand why Stella has become accustomed to Stanley's rude behaviour, why she tolerates it and is always ready to clean up the mess after the poker parties. She suggests leaving Stanley and opening a shop together with the help of Shep Huntleigh, a millionaire she pretends to have known since she was his girlfriend at the college. Blanche is upset and confused when she first wants to ring Shep up and then tries to write a letter of despair to him with her eyebrow pencil on a sheet of Kleenex. Stella laughs at her and offers her some money when Blanche tells her that she has only got some cents. Blanche underlines that she is not able to stay with Stanley any longer and takes it for granted that also Stella wants to leave him since she has been brought up in a different society at Belle Reve. Stella, however, admits that she feels sexually attracted to her husband and loves him.
Because of the noise of a train Stella and Blanche are not aware of Stanley appearing outside the house and overhearing their talk. Blanche describes Stanley as ordinary and primitive. In her opinion he is a survivor of the Stone Age and behaves like a wild beast in the jungle. She compares the poker players to a party of apes and underlines that Stanley is totally void of culture and tender feelings. When another train has passed noisily, Stanley enters, is embraced by his wife and grins at Blanche without showing his true feelings about what he has heard.

Scene Five

While Stella is dressing in the bedroom, Blanche is laughing nervously about the letter to Shep Huntley she has just finished because it is full of lies about her present situation. Suddenly they hear a row upstairs between Eunice and Steve because Eunice believes that her husband is unfaithful. She leaves the house to call the police but instead gets a drink in a bar when Steve appears with a bruise on his forehead and runs after his wife. Whilst Stanley is banging things around, Blanche wants to know his astrological sign and tells that she was born under Virgo, which makes Stanley laugh contemptuously because he has been informed about Blanche's life in Laurel where she stayed in a brothel-like hotel.

Eunice and Steve return after having made it up and Stanley leaves for the bowling alley. Blanche is upset and tells her sister that people are gossiping about her in Laurel. When Belle Reve was lost she had to be attractive and look for protection and alludes to the kindness of men who made love to her. Stella does not really listen to her but adds a shot of whisky to the coke as Blanche wishes.

Blanche expresses how grateful she is for her sister's kindness and tells her that she wants to make Mitch find her attractive and desire her because she needs security and that it is unbearable to stay with Stanley any longer.

After Stanley has called for Eunice, Steve and his wife, they leave for the bowling alley whereas Blanche stays behind. A young man who collects the money for the evening paper appears and Blanche behaves seductively and finally kisses him on the mouth and thus makes the young collector perplexed. She then asks him to go while saying that she would like to keep him but has to keep her hands off children. At the end of the scene Mitch appears with a bunch of roses which Blanche presses to her lips.

Scene Six

It is two hours after midnight when Blanche and Mitch return from their visit to the amusement park on Lake Pontchartrain. Mitch has won a plaster statue at a shooting gallery. Both are disappointed because they were unable to entertain each other and enjoy the evening. Blanche asks Mitch to unlock the door and tells him that she must soon leave her sister's apartment. She is astonished when Mitch asks if she allows kissing him, which he had done before in the park. Blanche tells him that she had to stop his sexual advances because as a single girl she would have run the risk to be lost. Mitch does not really understand what she means and tells her that he likes her more than anybody else.

As Stanley and Stella have not yet returned home, Blanche invites Mitch to come in for a drink. She asks him to sit down in the bedroom, searches for whisky, lights a candle instead of switching the light on and tries to be romantic using some French sentences Mitch does not understand. She even asks him in French if he would like to sleep with her. When she admires the shape and size of his body, he tells her that he is a member of the New Orleans Athletic Club. When they talk about their weight, Blanche asks him to lift her. But when Mitch hesitates to release her, he is told to treat her like a gentleman.

Mitch suggests that they should go out with Stanley and Stella one night and tells that he was in the army with Stanley. Blanche blames Stanley for being rude to her and offending her all the time. She complains about the lack of privacy in the small apartment and Stanley's uninhibited behaviour. She starts lying when she tells Mitch that she stays with her sister and Stanley for the summer because as a teacher with a low salary she cannot afford a holiday somewhere else. Mitch does not believe that Stanley hates her. When he wants to know her age because he talked about her to his mother without knowing how old Blanche is, Blanche is nervous and does not answer his question. Instead she wants to know more about Mitch's mother and learns that she is terminally ill and wants Mitch to marry before she dies. Blanche seems to be honest when she tells Mitch about her marriage when she was sixteen. She loved her young husband Allan very much but feels guilty that she did not help him when he needed her help. When she discovered his homosexual relationship to an older man, they pretended that nothing had happened and went to a dancing hall. But in the middle of the dance when she told Allan that he disgusts her, he suddenly ran away and shot himself. Mitch feels pity for her, embraces and kisses her. When he tells her that they need each other and alludes to marrying her, Blanche sobs and thanks God.

Scene Seven

Late in the afternoon in mid-September Stella is decorating the table for Blanche's birthday supper while Blanche is taking her usual hot bath. Stanley comes into the room and blames Blanche for permanently insulting him as common. Stella tries to explain to him that Blanche was brought up in different social circumstances. But Stanley replies that she has told them a lot of lies.

While Blanche is singing a popular song in the bathroom, Stanley tells his wife what he has learned about Blanche's life in Laurel. A supply-man of his firm, who frequently goes to Laurel, has told him that Blanche is well-known there because she lived like a prostitute in a hotel until the owner asked her to leave. When Stella does not believe that it is true, Stanley tells her that Blanche continued to have sex with soldiers from a nearby camp until she was told by the mayor of Laurel to leave the town. Moreover, she was dismissed from school because of her sexual relationship with a seventeen-year-old boy. Stella is still unable to believe the story about her sister and tells her husband about Blanche's love and marriage to a homosexual when she was very young and inexperienced.

Though Blanche is about thirty, Stella begins sticking twenty-five candles on the birthday cake to flatter her and tells Stanley that Mitch has been invited to come. But Stanley replies that she should not expect Mitch to come be-

cause as Mitch has been his friend since they were in the army together he has informed him about Blanche's life in Laurel. Consequently Mitch no longer wants to marry Blanche. When Stanley tells his wife that Blanche must leave them and that he has already bought a bus ticket for her, Stella despairs because she does not know what Blanche will do without a job.
When Stanley shouts at Blanche to get out of the bathroom, Blanche appears with a frightened look and tells her sister that she feels refreshed but soon recognizes that her sister is lying when she pretends that nothing has happened while she was having a bath.

Scene Eight

Three quarters of an hour later Stanley, Stella and Blanche are finishing the birthday supper in a sad and miserable mood. Blanche tries to cheer everybody up and hides her true feelings about having been stood up by Mitch. She asks Stanley to tell a joke or an amusing story but he denies knowing one that is refined enough. When Stella asks her to tell a story, she tells about a parrot that started swearing though its owner tried to prevent it. But she is the only one who laughs about the joke.
When Stanley eats the remaining chop with his fingers, Stella compares him with a pig and asks him to wash his fingers and help her to clear the table. Instead, Stanley smashes some dishes on the floor and shouts at Stella and Blanche never to insult him again calling him a pig, Polack or vulgar since he is the master in his home.
After Stanley has left to smoke a cigarette on the porch, Blanche asks Stella to tell her the truth why Mitch did not come to her birthday supper and decides to ring him up. While Stella reproaches her husband for his behaviour towards Blanche and starts crying, Blanche in vain tries to phone Mitch. Stanley comforts his wife telling her that they would be able to continue their way of life after the baby is born and Blanche has left.
Stella returns to the kitchen and lights the candles on the birthday cake. Blanche is delighted when she sees them and becomes poetic. She feels insulted by Mitch and stresses that she will not be taken for granted. When Stanley complains about the steam from the bathroom, Blanche explains that she needs hot baths for her nerves and insults Stanley again calling him a Polack without any nerves in his body. Stanley protests against it and tells her that people from Poland are called Poles and that he is an American citizen and proud of the country. After a short interruption by a phone call from a bowling partner, Stanley hypocritically tells Blanche that he has got a birthday present for her, a bus ticket back to Laurel. Blanche is shocked and runs into the bathroom. Stella is upset that her husband could be so cruel to her sister and tells him that she was a tender girl but finally abused by men like him. Stanley thinks that his behaviour is justified because after Stella's adapt-

ing to his way of life they have been happy together until Blanche turned up and insulted him. Suddenly Stella wishes to be taken to the hospital, obviously because of her labour pains. Finally Blanche comes out of the bathroom whispering Spanish lines.

Scene Nine

When Blanche is sitting in a bedroom chair and drinking whisky to forget her hopeless situation, Mitch turns up unshaven and in his work clothes. Blanche is excited and hides the whisky bottle in the closet and puts a bit of eau de cologne and powder on her face before she lets him enter. After a reproachful remark she offers him her lips which he ignores. When she tells him that she hears the polka music which was played before her young husband's death and that it stops when she hears the shot he fired when he committed suicide, Mitch believes that she is mad. He tells her that he did not want to see her but she pretends that she did not hear what he was saying and changes the subject by talking about her tidying the room. She offers him a drink, which he rejects because he does not want to take Stanley's whisky who has told him that she is a heavy drinker.
As the light is turned down, Mitch remarks that he has never seen her in full light. When he tears the paper lantern off the light bulb Blanche is frightened and tells him that she prefers magic to being realistic. But Mitch turns the light on to have a close look at her. When she cries out and covers her face, he turns the light off again and tells her that he does not mind that she is older than he thought but he checked what Stanley told him about her life in Laurel and found out that it is true. First she tries to deny everything but finally she tells the truth. She admits that she had sexual relationships with strangers after Allan's death because she felt lonely and was looking for protection. After her affair with a seventeen-year-old boy she was fired and did not know where to go but to her sister's home. She tells Mitch that she was grateful when she met him because contrary to the others he is gentle and she hoped to find peace with him. When Mitch reproaches her for having told lies, Blanche answers that she has never lied in her heart.
A blind Mexican woman selling tin flowers for funerals passes by and reminds Blanche of her life on the plantation with the dying relatives and her slipping out of the house to follow the calls of the young soldiers. But her attempt at arousing Mitch's compassion fails. Instead, his sexual desire is aroused and he tries to embrace Blanche to have sex with her. When she asks him to marry her, he tells her that she is not clean enough to be accepted by his mother. Blanche hysterically begins to scream fire and Mitch flees out of the apartment.

Scene Ten

A few hours later Blanche is drinking whisky and packing her belongings. After dressing herself in a white evening gown and putting her rhinestone tiara on her head in front of the mirror of the dressing table, she imagines to be admired by some men whom she invites to take a swim in the moonlight and warns them to dive and hit a rock since all of them are drunk. When she takes a hand mirror to look at herself more closely, she dislikes her look and smashes the mirror down.

Stanley, who is slightly drunk, enters in his bowling shirt and tells Blanche that the baby will not be born before morning. Blanche is afraid of being alone with Stanley and pretends to have received a telegram from Shep Huntleigh, her boy friend at the college, who has become a millionaire in the Dallas oil industry. She lies that he has invited her to take part in a cruise on his yacht. Though Blanche asks Stanley to close the curtains when he takes his shirt off, he does not care and opens a bottle of beer, which he pours over his head. He offers her the bottle, which she refuses, and asks her to make peace. He puts on his silk pyjamas while Blanche is looking forward to regaining privacy when she meets Shep Huntleigh since he is a gentleman who respects her. She tells that he feels lonely and wishes to see her because she is an intelligent and cultivated woman and though her physical beauty fades, the beauty of her mind and tenderness of her heart increases. She asks herself why she has been so silly to cast her pearls before swine, i.e. Stanley and Mitch, who dared to turn up in work clothes and repeat the slander about her. She tells the lie that after having thrown Mitch out of the apartment he returned with roses and asked her to forgive him. But she could not because deliberate cruelty is the one thing that cannot be forgiven. She goes on lying about her finishing the relationship with Mitch by telling that their ways of life and education are too different.

When Stanley asks her whether Mitch's visit was before or after she got Shep's telegram, Blanche gives herself away and Stanley recognizes that she has only told lies and did not receive a telegram, that there is no millionaire and Mitch did not come back with roses since he knows where he is. Blanche is shocked and does not know what to answer while Stanley continues to speak his mind and tells her that she looks ridiculous in her carnival outfit and has behaved in an arrogant way and permanently consumed his whisky. Blanche despairs and uses the telephone as if trying to ring up Shep Huntleigh and talking to the operator. Finally she cries for help when Stanley leaves the bathroom and puts the phone on the hook again.

When Stanley follows her into the bedroom, Blanche is terrified and warns him to thrust the top of a bottle into his face, which she has broken on the table. He grasps her wrist, forces her to drop the bottle top and carries her to the bed to rape her.

Scene Eleven

While Blanche is taking a bath Stella is crying and packing her sister's clothes into her trunk. Stanley and his friends are playing poker in the kitchen and when Pablo curses Stanley's good luck, he brags about his surviving in the war and tells that his maxim of life is to be always ahead in the rat race of life whereupon Mitch calls him a braggart and a bull.

Passing the poker table Eunice calls them callous and compares them to pigs. When she tells Stella that the baby is sleeping and that she has brought her some grapes, Stella replies that Blanche does not want to eat anything but has only asked for a drink. Moreover, she has told her that she is going to recover in the country, which Blanche believes to do with Shep Huntleigh. From the bathroom Blanche asks Stella to write the phone number down if anybody calls and put out a silk dress with a seahorse pin and artificial violets she wants to wear when she leaves.

Stella feels bad about lying to her sister and does not want to believe that Blanche told her the truth about being raped by her husband. If it were true she does not know how to go on living with him. Eunice advises her not to believe Blanche and to go on living whatever happens. When Blanche appears she asks whether she got a call from Shep Huntleigh. As Mitch is unable to concentrate on the poker game Stanley slaps him on the shoulder. Blanche is shocked and wants to know what is going on. To calm her Stella and Eunice tell her that she looks wonderful and is going on vacation. Blanche asks them to help her get dressed since she wants to leave as fast as possible.

But when Blanche is ready to leave she is pushed into a chair by Stella and Eunice because they have to wait until she will be called for. Blanche does not want to pass the poker table and imagines being on the sea where she would die holding the hand of a young ship's doctor and be dropped overboard in a white sack. When a doctor and a nurse ring the doorbell, the poker players stop talking, Stella tries to suppress her emotions and Eunice tells Blanche that the gentleman from Dallas has arrived. But when Blanche hears that there is also a lady waiting for her, she cannot imagine who she is and gets nervous. Stella and Eunice again confirm that she looks lovely when Blanche fearfully enters the kitchen.

When the Doctor greets her, Blanche is frightened because it is not Shep Huntleigh. She runs back to Stella and then into the bedroom looking for protection. Stanley and the Matron follow her and she pretends to have forgotten something. When Stanley tears the paper lantern from the light bulb and offers it to her, Blanche screams and tries to pass the Matron. Stella is upset and feels remorse for what she has done to her sister. Eunice tries to comfort her telling that Blanche can no longer stay with them. While the Matron holds Blanche's arm tightly to prevent her escape and Blanche defends herself wildly, Mitch accuses Stanley of being the cause of the disaster and hits him. Steve and Pablo stop him until Mitch collapses at the table.

Relationships between the Major Characters

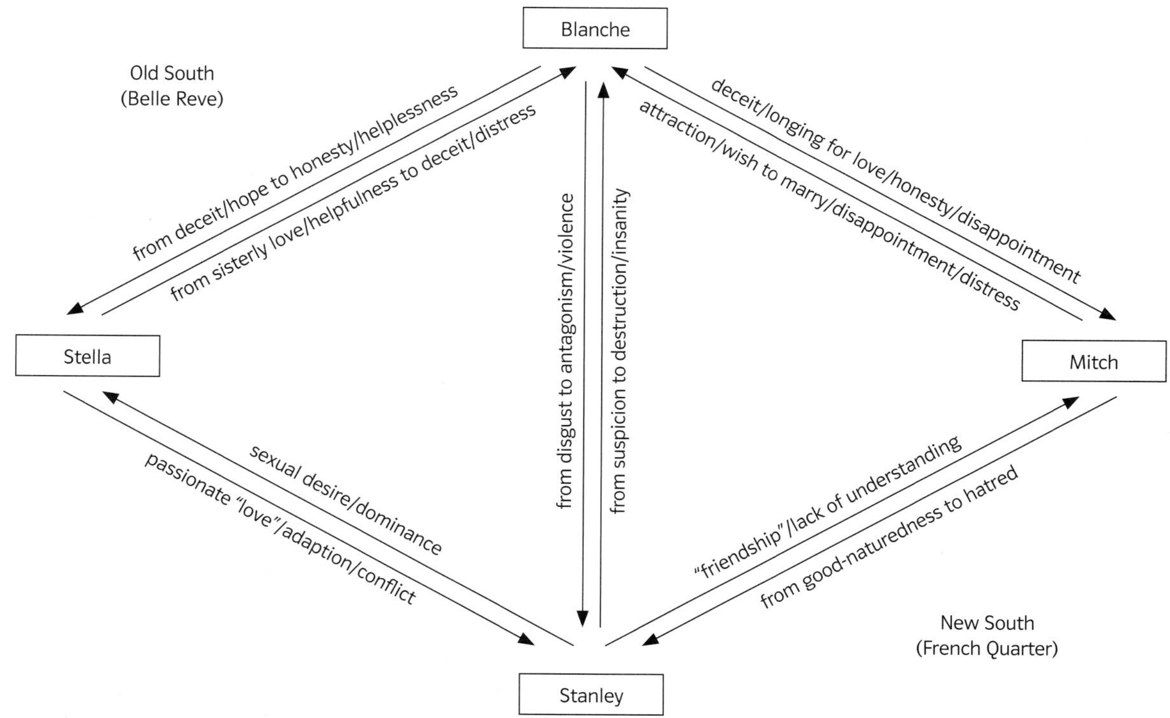

Finally the Doctor appears and addresses Blanche in a friendly and gentle way. He asks the Matron to let Blanche go, gentlemanlike offers Blanche his arm and leads her out of the bedroom. Blanche tells him that she has always depended on the kindness of strangers and walks out without looking back while Stella is crying and shouting her name. Eunice places the baby in Stella's arms. The poker players, who stood back when Blanche passed them, return to the poker table except Stanley who comforts his desperate wife in a voluptuous way. At the end of the play the poker game continues.

2. The Characters

The major characters of the play are Blanche, Stanley, Stella and Mitch, perhaps also Eunice since she plays an important role at the end of the play. According to Tennessee Williams, Blanche is the protagonist of the play because her tragic fate is the main topic. Stanley is her antagonist, whereas Stella's position is between her husband and her sister. She tries to find a compromise until she finally decides to deceive Blanche and to go on living with her husband. Mitch is Blanche's last hope but like Stanley and Stella he fails to accept her as she is.

2.1 Blanche DuBois

When Blanche meets Mitch the first time, she explains to him that her French name, Blanche DuBois, means "white woods. Like an orchard in spring!" (p. 41, ll. 21 f), which alludes to her vivid imagination. Her ancestors were French Huguenots who immigrated to America. She was brought up together with her younger sister Stella, who describes her as "tender and trusting" when she was a little girl (p. 84, l. 20) but also as unsteady which "caused sorrow at home. She was always – flighty" (p. 77, ll. 4 f). As their parents were rather wealthy and owned a plantation they belonged to a higher social class and attached great importance on good manners and education.
But her male relatives had sold most of the land belonging to the plantation piece by piece until only the house, about twenty acre of ground, a cemetery and lots of debts were left. They had always needed money for their extravagant and adulterous sex life and had brought themselves into disrepute. When Stella left the plantation to marry, Blanche stayed behind and had to care for her relatives who were terminally ill. As she felt lonely and desperate, she sometimes left the house at night to have sexual contacts with soldiers of a camp nearby. When all her relatives had died, she had to leave the plantation because she could not pay off the mortgage because her relatives had not left any money and she received only a "pitiful salary at the school" (p. 21, ll. 18 f). So Belle Reve was lost.

At the age of sixteen she had married a handsome and sensitive young man, who wrote poems and whom she adored. But when she discovered that he was homosexual and told him how much she despised him, he shot himself. Blanche is unable to forget that she did not help him when he most needed her help. She believes that her behaviour is unforgivable and is frequently haunted by the polka which was played before his death and by the shot she heard when he committed suicide. Her feeling guilty of his death seems to be the reason why she prefers white dresses and frequently takes a bath as if wishing to appear innocent and purifying herself from a sin. On the other hand Blanche does not only want to feel fresh because of the warm and humid climate in New Orleans but also tries to quiet her nerves by a hot bath because she feels anxious and is worried about her desperate situation.

After leaving the plantation Blanche stayed in a hotel in Laurel but was asked to move because of her sexual affairs. She also lost her job as an English teacher because she seduced a seventeen-year-old boy. Finally she was ordered to leave the town by the mayor. As she did not have any money and did not know how to survive, the only place she could go to was her sister's home in New Orleans.

Thus Tennessee Williams explains to a certain extent why Blanche went astray and enables the reader or theatregoer to understand her behaviour when she stays with Stella and her husband, meets Mitch and finally is taken to a mental hospital.

The dramatist introduces Blanche in the first scene of the play in a way that stresses her outward appearance as incongruous to the poor and run-down setting. Moreover, her disbelief that her sister lives in such miserable conditions and her offensive behaviour towards Eunice underline both her disappointment and her conceitedness though she herself is really destitute and is looking for a place to stay and find protection. She hides her real situation by her extravagant outfit. Tennessee Williams also alludes to her being addicted to drinking alcohol as a means to steady her nerves and her attempts at avoiding bright light to hide her real looks and true age. Her vivacity, embrace of her sister and her compliments seem to be exaggerated as if she had to hide her true thoughts and feelings. As she dislikes her sister's home but does not want to hurt her, she is uncertain how to behave and contradicts herself, when on the one hand she expresses that she finds Stella's home horrible and on the other hand tries to correct herself saying something nice about it. She lies to her sister when she pretends not to know where the whisky bottle is though she has just drunk of it and tries to make her believe that she is no alcoholic though she admits it a bit later, for instance by asking her to put the bottle away in order not to be tempted.

Blanche is eloquent and speaking so much that her sister is nearly unable to say anything. Instead of waiting for the questions of her sister, Blanche presumes that she wants to ask her what she herself is thinking of, for instance why she could leave school before the end of the term. She tells the truth in form of a question but then tells a lie, namely that she was not fired but that the high school superintendent allowed her to recover since she felt exhausted and needed a holiday. When her sister does not say anything about her appearance, Blanche asks her about her opinion and though she is flattered she reacts in a coquettish way: "God love you for a liar! Daylight never exposed so total a ruin!" (p. 17, ll. 8 f) Thus she indirectly admits why she is afraid of being seen in bright light since she looks older than she wants to appear. That is why she never goes out with Mitch in daylight and asks him to put a paper lantern on the light bulb. She tells Mitch that magic is more important to her than being realistic: "I don't want realism. [...] I'll tell you what I want. Magic! [...] I try to give that to people. I misrepresent things to them. I don't tell the truth, I tell what *ought* to be truth. And if that is sinful, then let me be damned for it!" (p. 89, ll. 12 ff) Thus she is not willing to accept a reality she dislikes but tries to establish or hold on a reality she imagines and would like to be real.

As she knows that her beauty is fading, she is frequently asking if she looks nice or is fishing for compliments, even if the answers are not true or she is cheated by her sister and Eunice at the end of the play. She is shocked when Mitch sees her in bright light and realizes that she looks older than she pretends to be. Stanley is the only person who dislikes flattering her and also does not react when she tries to flirt with him (cf. p. 29, ll. 16 ff). But in Scene Ten she underlines her inner values and tells him: "Physical beauty is passing. A transitory possession. But beauty of the mind and richness of the spirit and tenderness of the heart – and I have all of those things – aren't taken away, but grow! Increase in the years!" (p. 96, ll. 6 ff) Blanche cannot only be considered as a liar and promiscuous woman. She is also presented as a person who insists on maintaining values the other characters are not able to recognize.

From the very beginning of the play she seems to be nervous, mentally unstable and insecure, for instance when laughing nervously or telling Stella that she looks plump but corrects herself by saying that it suits her and then tells her that she has put on weight around the hips and should be careful. She even orders Stella to stand up and change her hair cut and treats her like a little child playing the role of an elder sister. Stella believes that Blanche seems "a little bit nervous or overwrought or something" (p. 19, ll. 1 f) and asks her to stop her "hysterical outburst" (p. 20, l. 17) when Blanche alludes to the loss of Belle Reve. When Blanche insinuates that Stella wants to accuse her of the loss of the plantation though her sister does not know anything about it and is just listening, Blanche wallows in self-pity and relentlessly blames Stella for having left her alone. Finally she becomes insulting which makes her sister cry.

Before meeting Stanley, Blanche already feels uneasy because Stella describes him vaguely as "a different species" (p. 19, l. 8) and his friends as "a mixed

lot" (p. 18, l. 29). Blanche, however, offensively calls Stanley and his friends "Polacks" (p. 18, l. 28; p. 21, l. 26) or "a party of apes" (p. 54, l. 2). She is prejudiced against immigrants coming from Poland or Ireland (cf. p. 18, ll. 19 f), obviously because they were poor and – as she believes – also uneducated.
Throughout the play she is easily frightened, in the first scene for instance of Stanley, because she does not know how he will react when he meets her since her sister did not tell him that she would come and stay with them. She is frightened of shrieking cats and shocked when Stella returns to her husband though he has beaten her. Finally she panics because Stanley is going to rape her and at the end of the play she panics because she feels being caught in a trap. On the other hand Blanche also shows some courage when she protects her sister against Stanley's violence or threatens to thrust a broken bottle into Stanley's face, when he intends to rape her. At the end of the play she fights with the Matron who tries to subdue her.
When Stanley arrives and discovers that there is less whisky in the bottle than before, Blanche lies that she rarely touches alcohol. As she feels that Stanley is strong-willed and direct, she does not dare to protest against his taking off his shirt though she always insists on good manners and privacy. When Stanley asks questions about her job and her marriage, she gives evasive answers and feels sick. When Stanley urges her to tell the truth and give him the papers about the loss of the plantation, she first criticizes that "life is too full of evasions and ambiguities" and then lies that she only likes strong colours instead of "pinks and creams". But finally she consents and wants to finish the "double-talk" (cf. p. 30, ll. 26 ff). But after having given all the papers about Belle Reve to Stanley, she insincerely tells her sister that she had "laughed and treated it all as a joke" but also tells the truth that she had flirted with him. Though she resents her sister's marriage to such an uncultivated and ill-mannered man, she tells her that "maybe he's what we need to mix with our blood now that we've lost Belle Reve and have to go on without Belle Reve to protect us" (p. 34, ll. 21 ff). Blanche's ambiguous and contradictory words underline her insecurity and her desire to find a place where she could stay and find protection.
It remains doubtful whether her happiness and good humour she sometimes shows can be taken seriously, for instance her joy when she arrives and embraces Stella, which seems to be exaggerated. When she sees the building in which her sister lives, her humour is "faintly hysterical" (p. 12, l. 27) and when she leaves with her for a night out, she is first frightened of the sudden shouts of the tamale vendor but then starts laughing breathlessly, which changes to a "desperate laughter" (p. 34, ll. 32 f). But sometimes she is joking (cf. p. 61, l. 28) when she meets the young collector or laughing when she ridicules the looks of the wives of Stanley's friends (cf. p. 38, l. 38). She rather frequently treats Stanley in an ironical way, e.g. when she tells him that "we

ladies are cordially *not* invited!" (p. 29, l. 10) to the poker party or calls him "my loving brother-in-law" (p. 89, ll. 27 f). When she is stood up by Mitch at her birthday supper, she pretends not to care and tells a parrot joke she believes is funny. But she is the only one who laughs about it, which reminds of gallows humour. She is even able to laugh about her own silly behaviour when she reads her letter to Shep Huntleigh (cf. p. 55, ll. 2 ff). But her humorous behaviour mostly seems artificial in order to hide or play down her true thoughts and feelings about her desperate situation.
She frequently insults Stanley, because she detests his behaviour and table manners as rude and uncivilized and states: "I have been foolish – casting my pearls before swine!" (p. 96, ll. 13 f) She calls him a madman, Polack, pig, disgusting, vulgar and describes him as bestial, ape-like and as a survivor of the Stone Age (cf. p. 53, l. 25 – p. 54, l. 12). That is why she cannot understand why her sister despite her being brought up differently does not want to leave him but tolerates his macho-like behaviour and even desires him after having been beaten by him instead of running away with her and settle down somewhere else.
She is astonished that her sister has no maid but nevertheless does not help her with the household work though she later pretends to do so in order to win Mitch's sympathy. She likes to be served by Stella as if she were her servant. Blanche insists on good manners and wants Stanley and his friends to be polite and behave like gentlemen though she must realize that they do not care very much about her "old-fashioned ideals" (cf. p. 68, l. 22) apart from Mitch before he gets to know about her real life in Laurel. She sometimes behaves in a conceited way and feels superior to the other people because she belongs to an "aristocratic" family of plantation owners and as an English teacher her educational level is rather high whereas the other characters are more or less uneducated and unable to appreciate art, music and literature. But in fact she is desperately looking for a place to stay in order to find peace and protection since the plantation is lost and she is destitute and without a job.
When she recognizes that it is impossible to stay with Stanley and her sister, she hopes to marry Mitch. She is willing to adapt to his way of life and therefore behaves seductively to make him desire and marry her. "I want to *deceive* him enough to make him – want me" (p. 60, ll. 21 f). But before Mitch arrives with a bunch of roses to meet her for a night out, she treats a young man seductively who appears to collect the money for the evening paper. He seems to remind her of the seventeen-year-old student she had seduced in Laurel or also of her late husband. She imagines that he looks like a young Prince of the Arabian Nights and kisses him on his mouth but then realizes that she has to be good and keep her "hands off children" (cf. p. 62, l. 39). This episode not only shows that Blanche has not yet overcome her past life but that her desire for sex and love is still strong. When she tells Mitch about her

miserable life on the plantation caring for her dying mother, she says: "Death [...] We didn't dare even admit we had ever heard of it! [...] The opposite is desire." (p. 91, ll. 16 ff)

When she is unmasked and even her honesty does not change Mitch's mind, she retreats into the dream world of meeting a "real" gentleman, i.e. Shep Huntleigh, her former friend at the college who – as she imagines – has become a millionaire and has invited her to a Caribbean cruise on his yacht. She believes that he is her last hope to escape the "trap" of Stanley's home since Mitch refused to marry her after he had been informed about her immoral past. Moreover, she knows that returning to Laurel with the ticket Stanley cynically gave her as a birthday present is impossible. Instead, her nervous and insecure behaviour gradually turns into a state of insanity when all her evasions, tricks, half-truths and lies no longer help her to hide the truth and to look for security and protection. But even her honesty does not help though she tells Mitch that she had so many affairs with strangers because she was hunting for some protection and hoped to find it with him since he is gentle and both are lonely and need somebody to be settled and come to peace (cf. p. 90, ll. 11 ff). Moreover, Blanche denies that she lied: "Don't say I lied to you. [...] Never inside, I didn't lie in my heart." (p. 90, ll. 29 ff) When she lies to Stanley that Mitch asked her to forgive him, she tells him that she could not because "deliberate cruelty is not forgivable. It is the one unforgivable thing in my opinion and it is the one thing of which I have never, never been guilty." (p. 96, ll. 24 ff) Her statement may be true in general but she was at least once cruel in her life when she did not try to understand and help her young husband who then committed suicide.

There are many allusions to her nervous condition, hysterical behaviour and sudden fears until she appears to be more and more confused and mentally deranged and finally is considered insane. After Mitch's attempt at raping her she panics. When she is alone with Stanley in Scene Ten she is horrified since she feels trapped and is finally raped though she desperately tries to defend herself. In the last scene of the play she is terribly frightened, hysterical and shocked. She seems to be unable to distinguish between what is real and what is illusion and still believes that Shep Huntleigh will fetch her to accompany him on a Caribbean cruise. She imagines smelling the sea and wishes to die on the ocean. She then mixes up everything, for instance Eunice's grapes as the reason of her death because she eats them unwashed, a young ship's doctor, who holds her hand and owns a big silver watch, which reminds of Mitch's silver case. Moreover, she wants to be dropped overboard in a clean white sack "into an ocean as blue as [...] my first lover's eyes" (cf. p. 103, ll. 34 f). In an interview of 1974 (cf. *Conversations*, pp. 276 f) Tennessee Williams states that Blanche's insanity at the end of the play metaphorically expresses that she was broken by society. She "had personal, great strength and personal vulnerability that was finally broken. [...] She was not adaptable

to the circumstances as they were, that the world had imposed on her. She was a sacrificial victim, you know; she was metaphorical as a sacrificial victim of society."
When Blanche is finally deceived by her sister, who tells her that she is going on vacation, and by the gentlemanlike behaviour of the Doctor who takes her to the mental hospital, she leaves in a way that stresses her human dignity. But her final words to the Doctor, which underline her being disoriented, lonely and helpless but trusting, are: "Whoever you are – I have always depended on the kindness of strangers." (p. 107, ll. 35 f)

To sum up, as Blanche is a very complex character whom the other characters are unable to understand and accept. There are various contradictions in her own nature, such as her sexual desire and her longing for love and protection, her refined self, politeness and education versus her prejudices and insulting behaviour, her being a liar and honest, her feeling superior to others and her self-deceit and illusion, which to a large extent contrasts with the people in the French Quarter and the ordinary life they are used to live. Tennessee Williams underlines that "it is not the essential dignity but the essential ambiguity of man that I think needs to be stated" (*Essays*, p. 118) and describes Blanche both as a fragile "moth" and as "a delicate tigress with her back to the wall" (*Essays*, p. 153). Blanche makes use of contradictory and desperate means to find a safe place and maintain her individual dignity in a hostile society.
By alluding to Ernest Hemingway's statement "A man can be destroyed but not defeated" in his story *The Old Man and the Sea* (1952) the playwright states that "she's a tiger, extreme tigers are destroyed, not defeated" (*Conversations*, p. 277). He also believes that despite the rat race in modern society "there exists in some persons a sensibility to the unfortunate situations of others, a capacity for concern and compassion" (*Essays*, p. 50), which might also be felt with Blanche.

2.2 Stanley Kowalski

Stanley is Blanche's antagonist. His ancestors were Polish immigrants and contrary to Blanche, who represents the decaying aristocratic Old South of French plantation owners, he works as an auto-parts salesman and thus belongs to the generation of the new industrialized South. He is fond of bowling and playing poker with his friends in his spare time, which seems to be characteristic of the working class. He is proud of being an American patriot and fought in Italy in the Second World War together with his friend Mitch. "I am not a Polack. People from Poland are Poles, not Polacks. But what I am is a one hundred percent American, born and raised in the greatest country on earth and proud as hell of it [...]" (p. 83, ll. 12 ff).

Contrary to Blanche, who guesses that he is "not so highbrow" but "primitive" and "sub-human", Stella is convinced of his being rather intelligent and that he will get on in his job since he is "the only of his crowd that's likely to get anywhere" (p. 38, ll. 19 f). Stanley is clever and suspicious and easily finds out that Blanche tries to deceive him and tells lies. He frequently treats her ironically to allude to her dishonesty or illusions, for instance when he exclaims "What poetry!" (p. 82, l. 37). His birthday present shows that he can also be cynical and laugh about unlucky people such as the "human bottle-opener" who lost his front teeth (cf. p. 95, l. 11). On the other hand he enjoys joking and laughing with his friends about dirty jokes mainly.
Stanley is convinced of being the master in his own house and macho-like reminds his wife of his superiority when she dares to criticize him: "Remember what Huey Long said – 'Every Man is a King!' And I am the king around here, so don't forget it!" (p. 81, ll. 27 ff) He dominates his wife, pays the bills and does not give her regular pocket-money. He also treats his friends in an authoritarian way since he believes to be the "team-captain" (p. 83, l. 28). He cannot stand losing at cards but gets angry if he does (cf. Scene Three). But when he wins at cards at the end of the play and Pablo curses his luck he starts boasting: "You know what luck is? Luck is believing you're lucky. Take at Salerno [where the American troops landed during World War II]. I believed I was lucky. I figured that 4 out of 5 would not come through but I would ... and I did. I put that down as a rule. To hold front position in this rat-race you've got to believe you are lucky." (p. 100, ll. 15 ff)
If anybody does not follow his orders or wishes he gets hot-tempered and violent, for instance when he smashes his dishes instead of carrying them to the kitchen as Stella asked him. She seems to tolerate his behaviour when she tells Blanche that Stanley had smashed all the light bulbs with one of her slippers on their wedding night. Stanley also commands when and how to play poker and is enraged if anything is on the poker table except cards, chips and whisky and insults his poker friends if they protest. He is insensitive to other people's feelings and does not feel compassion with Mitch who takes care of his sick mother but feels disturbed by his emotions and calls him a cry-baby. He also feels disturbed by the rumba music Blanche wants to hear and throws the radio out of the window. He even hits his pregnant wife when she calls him a drunkard and asks his poker friends to go home. But when he is subdued by his friends he calms down and remorsefully begins to sob and desperately shouts her name to make her return and spend the night with him. As Stella confirms, he easily gets furious if he is drunk but behaves like a lamb if he is sober again.
Contrary to Blanche's demand to behave like a gentleman and respect her privacy, Stanley's manners are impolite and rude. He does not care if his way of undressing or eating is indecent. Corresponding to his low social standard he uses colloquial American English or slang and is content that Stella has

adapted to his way of life to a large extent: “When we first met, me and you, you thought I was common. How right you was, baby. I was common as dirt. You showed me the snapshot of the place with the columns [Belle Reve], I pulled you down off them columns and how you loved it, having them colored lights going! And wasn't we happy together, wasn't it all okay till she showed here?” (p.84, ll. 31 ff) Thus Stanley reminds his wife of their living together before Blanche arrived and made it impossible to have sex as they were used to. Already at the beginning of the play Tennessee Williams describes Stanley as a “gaudy seed-bearer” (p. 22, l. 30) since sex is of vital importance to him and he behaves “with the power and pride of a richly feathered male bird among hens.” (p. 22, ll. 24 f)

When Stanley meets Blanche the first time, he is rather friendly to her and does not seem to care very much about her intention to stay with them. But as he is open-minded and realistic, he soon begins to dislike Blanche's affected behaviour and mistrusts her since he easily finds out that she tries to deceive him when she tells him that she does not know where the whisky bottle is. As he does not believe Blanche that Belle Reve is lost, he underlines that according to the Napoleonic Code he owns what his wife possesses, he demands to be shown the papers and begins to get information about her and her life in Laurel. As a salesman he obviously knows several people and experts who can inform him and are also able to give an opinion on the value of her jewellery. Stanley remains suspicious of Blanche throughout the play and finally tells her: “I've been on to you from the start! Not once did you pull any wool over this boy's eyes!” (p. 97, ll. 13 f). He does not want to be deceived and told lies by Blanche and is only interested in facts and the truth. He is characterized as honest, reliable and faithful to his friends since he also opens Mitch's eyes to the truth and thus destroys Blanche's hope to marry him. But he is also a contradictory character since he deceives his wife and Blanche when he behaves as if he did not overhear Blanche's accusations in Scene Four. He is dishonest to Stella when he does not tell her about the rape of her sister but intends to continue his family life based on deceit, as if nothing worth mentioning has happened.

Stanley regards Blanche as an intruder who endangers the life he is used to live with Stella and decides to get rid of her. He cynically gives her a ticket back to Laurel as a birthday present. When Stella is in hospital to give birth to their baby and Stanley and Blanche are alone at night the first time, Stanley tells Blanche that “we've had this date with each other from the beginning” (p. 99, ll. 24 f). Tennessee Williams seems to allude to the fact that Stanley has subconsciously desired Blanche before he rapes her and thus also demonstrates his superiority the only way he knows. Blanche, who flirts with Stanley in Scene Two, might also have supposed that Stanley desired her when in Scene Six (p. 69, ll. 33 ff) she says to Mitch: “Of course there is such a thing as the hostility of – perhaps in some perverse kind of a way he – No! To think of it makes me ... (*She makes a gesture of revulsion. [...]*).” At the end of the play Stanley does not feel any remorse or pity for Blanche when she is taken to the mental institution. But he seems to feel compassion for his wife and caresses her when she is distressed about her deceitful behaviour towards her sister.

2.3 Stella Kowalski

Though Stella has been brought up at Belle Reve, she leaves the plantation to marry Stanley who belongs to a lower class. Obviously because of their strong sexual relationship, she tolerates his uncouth manners and accepts his domineering role to a certain extent. Though he is hot-tempered and easily gets furious and even beats her when he had too much alcohol, she feels attached to him since he becomes kind again and caresses her after his uncontrolled outbreaks of anger. She feels lonely as soon as Stanley is not with her and loves him passionately.

She is really happy to see Blanche again and is considerate and kind towards her since she patiently listens to her, turns off the light when Blanche asks her for it and pours whisky in her tumbler when she realizes that her sister’s hand is shaking. When Blanche alludes to Stella’s poor living conditions, she replies that “it’s not that bad at all! New Orleans isn’t like other cities.” (p. 16, ll. 11 f) Stella appears to be rather quiet and peaceful because she does not protest against Blanche’s criticism of her apartment, her weight, her falling in love with Stanley only because of his decorations and her being addressed like a little child but remains calm. She honestly tells her that Stanley and his friends are not lovely as Blanche believes and that she desires her husband and feels lonely when he is not with her.

But when Blanche reproaches her of having left Belle Reve without helping her to care for her dying relatives but only returned for the funerals and finally insults her and her husband, Stella is deeply hurt and starts crying. Nevertheless she understands her sister’s nervous and hysterical behaviour and does not feel insulted when her sister treats her like a little child and criticizes her appearance. Contrary to Blanche’s eloquence, she is rather silent and patient. As she knows that her sister needs being flattered, she asks her husband to be nice to her and admire her beauty and her dress. She defends her sister when Stanley becomes suspicious about the loss of Belle Reve and accuses Blanche of swindling them. She also tries to convince Stanley that Blanche’s clothes and jewellery are inexpensive and have been owned by her for a long time. As she wants to be kind to Blanche and help her overcome her depression and cheer her up, she asks Stanley for some money to go to a fashionable restaurant and after that to a show.

Because of her mild character Stella mostly tolerates Stanley’s behaviour and the rows of her neighbours. She spontaneously helps and supports her sister and encourages her when she doubts that Mitch will marry her. As she knows

that Blanche wants to hide her true age, she only puts twenty-five candles on the birthday cake to please her. But in order to protect herself Stella does not listen to Blanche when she describes her despair: "I don't listen to you when you are being morbid!" (p. 59, ll. 5 f) She also does not consent when Blanche criticizes her husband. When Stanley tells her about Blanche's life in Laurel, Stella does not want to hear any more. Thus she does not really want to understand her sister's feelings and to know the truth but seems to deceive herself.
Despite the rude and uncivilized behaviour of her husband and her neighbours, Stella has remained sensitive and not given up everything she was brought up to. Blanche's arrival seems to have revived conventional ideas about good manners. Thus she asks her husband to be polite to Blanche and dislikes it when Stanley whacks her on the thigh in front of people. She even dares to criticize his table manners and his cruelty towards Blanche and asks the poker players to leave if they "have one spark of decency" in them (cf. p. 43, l. 12). On the other hand she believes that her sister's superior attitude towards her husband is out of place.
Stella seems to be drawn between her husband and her sister to a certain extent and tries her best to find a way to live together. She for instance tells Stanley that Blanche was a tender girl and had to suffer terribly when she cared for her sick relatives to make him change his mind about her. Stella defends her sister against her husband's rudeness, criticizes his uncivilized behaviour and finally desperately asks him what Blanche shall do without their help and why he is so cruel to give Blanche a ticket back to Laurel as a birthday present. On the other hand Stella tries to explain to Blanche that they have to tolerate each other's habits and that Stanley is a rough diamond since he behaves violently when he is drunk or feels cheated but is soft afterwards and that she desires and loves him. But all her attempts at finding a compromise between Stanley and Blanche fail and she has to decide whether to leave Stanley or to make her sister go away.
As Stella is realistic enough to recognize that she is financially dependent on her husband and her sister's idea of setting themselves up in life with the help of Shep Huntleigh is absurd, she rejects Blanche's plan and finally decides not to risk her family life. As Blanche seems to become insane, she paves the way for Blanche being taken to a mental hospital without telling her about it. At the beginning of the play Stella does not react to Blanche's words when she tells her that she flirted with Stanley and at the end of the play she is also not willing to believe Blanche that her husband has raped her. She deceives her sister and herself because she does not want to leave her husband but follows Eunice's advice: "Don't ever believe it. Life has to go on. No matter what happens, you've got to keep on going." (p. 101, ll. 25 f)
Stella feels remorse about how she treated her sister and despairs. Her last words are: "Oh, God, what have I done to my sister?" (p. 106, ll. 32 f) She

desperately shouts Blanche's name. But she seems to be comforted by her husband when he caresses her.

2.4 Harold Mitch(ell)

Like Stanley and Blanche Mitch is about thirty years old and one of Stanley's friends, who play poker together and go to the bowling alley. During the Second World War Mitch and Stanley were in the same Engineers Corps and after that they have been working at the same factory. Mitch is a member of the New Orleans Athletic Club and likes swimming and keeping himself fit. He is big and tough but clumsy with women.

He loves his mother and cares for her since she is seriously ill. He remembers the girl who was his first and only love and as she died young he feels lonely. Though he is a bit clumsy and does not really know how to entertain women, he seems to be a sensitive and rather gentlemanlike character.

When Mitch sees Blanche the first time while she is taking off her blouse and is standing in the light through the curtains, he is no longer able to concentrate on the poker game. He is fascinated by Blanche and does not listen to Stanley's orders and shouts when he meets her. Blanche begins to flirt with Mitch by asking him for a cigarette and expresses her sympathy when he tells her that he got the silver case from a girl who died. He confirms her view that sorrow makes people sincere and listens to Blanche's fanciful explanation of her name, follows her wish to fasten a paper lantern over the light bulb, and wants to know whether she is married and what her profession is. Blanche only tells him half the truth and obviously succeeds in impressing him with her literary knowledge.

As Mitch is compassionate and peaceful, he helps to subdue and calm Stanley when he gets furious and hits Stella. He is gentle and considerate towards women when he repeats that "poker shouldn't be played in a house with women" (p. 43, l. 32 and p. 44, ll. 20 f). On the other hand he understands that Stanley and Stella are "crazy about each other" (p. 46, ll. 2 f) and tries to comfort Blanche, who is terrified by Stanley's violence and Stella's desire to spend the night with him.

When Mitch and Blanche return from a night out, Mitch feels depressed because he could not amuse Blanche. Though he desires her he is shy and asks her for a kiss and wants her to tell him if he goes too far. He alludes to marrying her since his mother wishes him to be settled before she dies. As Mitch feels lonely, Blanche tells him about the death of her young husband and her being lonely too. When Blanche begins to sob, Mitch draws her into his arms and compassionately says: "You need somebody. And I need somebody, too. Could it be – you and me, Blanche?" (p. 72, ll. 3 ff)

As long as Mitch does not know anything about Blanche's promiscuous life in Laurel, he is fascinated by Blanche and even says: "I like you to be exactly the

way that your are, because in all my – experience – I have never known anyone like you" (p. 65, ll. 32 f) and "I told my mother how nice you were, and I liked you" (p. 70, l. 11). But he is not really able to understand Blanche and accept her as she is after being informed about her by Stanley. He is unable to love Blanche really with all her weaknesses, faults and flaws but seems to be driven by blind desire. He is mother's boy and not self-reliant enough to overcome his mother's and his own conventional views.
After Blanche has been stood up by him at her birthday supper, Mitch meets her and ignores her friendliness she pretends. He is no longer considerate but ill-mannered since he appears in work clothes, is unshaven and has drunk alcohol. He is impolite and rudely tears the paper lantern from the light bulb to see her face in bright light. When Blanche admits that she hears the polka tune that was played before Allan shot himself, Mitch assumes that she is mad. He states that he does not bother whether she is older than she told him but that he is disappointed of her insincerity. Stanley has informed him about Blanche's life in Laurel and he also verified it by a supply-man who travels through Laurel and a merchant who knows Blanche. Though she honestly describes her despairing situation in Laurel and her wish for protection, he no longer believes her and finally even tries to rape her.
At the end of the play Mitch is unable to bear how Blanche is treated and accuses Stanley of being responsible for it: "You! You done this, all o' your God damn rutting with things you – [...] I'll kill you!" (p. 107, ll. 5 ff) When he tries to beat Stanley, he is held back by Steve and "collapses at the table, sobbing" (p. 107, l. 12) Thus Tennessee Williams stresses Mitch's despair by his violent attack and his emotional breakdown.

2.5 Eunice and Steve Hubbell

Eunice and Steve are the owners of the house, in which they occupy the upstairs apartment and Stella and Stanley the downstairs flat. Eunice is Stella's friend and accommodates her, when she was beaten by Stanley and fled to her. She also takes care of Stella's baby at the end of the play. When Blanche arrives, she is friendly to her and lets Blanche wait in Stella's apartment until she returns with Stella, though she feels offended by Blanche.
Contrary to Stella, Eunice is a resolute woman who does not allow her husband to dominate her. She blames him when he is late and orders him to come home immediately from the poker party. When she feels deceived by him with a blonde, she gets furious, starts a row and hurts him. But though she threatens to call the police, she meets her husband in a bar to have a drink together before they return arm in arm as if nothing has happened. Like the relationship between Stanley and Stella her relationship to her husband is mainly based on sex. As Stella has become accustomed to Eunice's and Steve's regular quarrels, the two couples live together as good neighbours.

Eunice blames Stanley heavily when he beats his pregnant wife and insults him furiously. As she does not know any other solution of the problem, she supports Stella's decision to let Blanche be taken to a mental hospital. She comforts her, places the baby in her arms and tells her that life must go on whatever happened.
Steve is Stanley's friend and takes part in his poker parties. He likes to crack dirty jokes, teases Mitch and contrary to Stanley tolerates Blanche's wish to listen to music. He helps to subdue Stanley when he gets furious and protests against the way Blanche is treated and deceived: "This is no way to do it. She should've been told." (p. 107, l. 1) But finally he deals another hand to continue playing poker as if nothing has happened.

2.6 The minor characters and walk-on parts

Stanley's poker friends Steve and Pablo appear to be rather "common" but on the other hand try to calm Stanley when he is furious and protest against Blanche's deceitful treatment at the end of the play.
In his stage directions Tennessee Williams describes the Doctor and the Matron who take Blanche to the mental hospital as the representatives of the "state institution with its cynical detachment" (p. 104, l. 1). The Matron is a "sinister figure" and "divested of all the softer properties of womanhood" (p. 105, ll. 35 f). She is strong and heartless and relentlessly wrestles Blanche to the ground and asks if she shall put her in a straitjacket. The Doctor, however, finally behaves like a gentleman and thus deceives Blanche to believe that she is going on a holiday.
The young collector appears only once to underline Blanche's soft spot for young men.
The other minor characters such as a black woman, a tamale vendor and a sailor contribute to the multiracial and multicultural background of New Orleans and to New Orleans as a seaport where careless people are easily cheated. A Mexican woman selling flowers to the dead is a symbol of death, which is an essential experience of Blanche whereas the other characters do not seem to care about it. Some walk-on parts, e.g. a prostitute and a policeman, help to convey an authentic impression of the night life in New Orleans and also contribute to the play's atmosphere of violence and crime.
Some people such as Blanche's late husband Allan Grey and Shep Huntleigh, whom Blanche imagines to accompany on a Caribbean cruise, do not appear on the stage but are referred to in order to understand Blanche's guilty conscience and her dream of wealth and protection.

To sum up, the major characters, Blanche, Stanley, Stella and Mitch, are round characters or psychologically complex characters with contradictory traits and emotions. Blanche is certainly the protagonist whose behaviour

and fate is meant to arouse the readers' or spectators' understanding and compassion. Also Eunice, Steve and Pablo are not really flat characters since they do not behave in a stereotype way but can be joking, violent and peaceful. The other characters are rather flat characters.
Some critics complained that the major characters in *A Streetcar Named Desire* are ambiguous and too complex, which is the reason of different interpretations. But in an essay of 1955 Tennessee Williams replies that this is quite natural.

> "Some mystery should be left in the revelation of character in a play, just as a great deal of mystery is always left in the revelation of character in life, even in one's own character to himself. [...] Was Blanche DuBois a liar? She told many lies in the course of *Streetcar* and yet at heart she was truthful." (*Essays*, p. 72)

III Analysis and Interpretation

1. The Play's Epigraph

Tennessee Williams insisted on having four lines of the poem "The Broken Tower" by Hart Crane precede the play. He identified with Hart Crane (1899–1932), who was his favourite poet, since Crane had also experienced a rather unhappy childhood and was homosexual and dependent on alcohol. He committed suicide. The four lines are probably chosen as a motto to *A Streetcar Named Desire* because they seem to allude to Blanche's "broken world" and desire for love which ends in despair. In his *Memoirs* (p. 204) he also describes his long depression after Frank Merlo's death as a "retreat into the broken world of my self" and mentions Hart Crane several times as a congenial poet. He even states that he himself is "as much of an hysteric as [...] Blanche; a codicil to my will provides for the disposition of my body in this way. 'Sewn up in a clean white sack and dropped over board, twelve hours north of Havana, so that my bones may rest not too far from those of Hart Crane'" (*Memoirs*, p. 117; cf. *Streetcar*, p. 103, ll. 32 ff).

2. The Title of the Play

When Tennessee Williams went to New Orleans in 1947 he continued writing a play whose first draft he had called *The Moth* when he was in Chicago. The title refers to Blanche's appearance and fragile character, which the playwright describes in the stage directions of the first scene: "There is something about her uncertain manner, as well as her white clothes, that suggests a moth." (p. 12, ll. 23 ff) But then he chose the title *Blanche's Chair in the Moon*, which seems to allude to the beginning of the ninth scene after Blanche was stood up by Mitch. The playwright obviously wanted to stress Blanche's loneliness and probably her living in an imaginary world. The third and fourth titles Tennessee Williams took into consideration were *The Primary Colors* and *The Poker Night*, which refer to the poker players (cf. *Streetcar*, Scene Three). Though he kept *The Poker Night* as the title of the third scene, he thought it inadequate for the whole play since it only refers to playing poker as a contrasting action to the central action of Blanche's fate. Another working title of the play was *Paper Lantern* (cf. *Letters*, p. 81), which stresses Blanche's fear of bright light, her trying to hide her true age and her love of magic.
When he stayed in the French Quarter in New Orleans, Tennessee Williams lived in a second-floor apartment in Dick Orme's house on the corner of St.

Peter and Royal streets during the winter 1947. Below him two streetcars with the final stops Desire and Cemeteries ran up and down Royal Street tracks (cf. Leavitt, p. 72).

The names of the trams inspired the playwright to mention them in his play when Blanche arrives at her sister's home in Elysian Fields Street. Both the trams and the street are used symbolically since desire is a major characteristic of the major characters and Cemeteries and Elysian Fields seem to foreshadow Blanche's tragic end. When Tennessee Williams had finished the play in Key West, he sent it to his representative Audrey Wood with its final title *A Streetcar Named Desire*.

3. The Stage Directions

Tennessee Williams introduces into the scenes of the play by rather long and detailed stage directions and also gives numerous instructions throughout the play. Thus the stage director, the actors, readers and critics of the play are informed about the dramatist's ideas of the setting, the action, the cast and how to play the roles, the costumes, light and sound effects, etc. The stage directions can also be compared with the stage productions in order to find out to what extent and possibly why they deviate from the playwright's views. The stage directions help understand the playwright's ideas because the dialogue of the characters is frequently ambiguous. The reader must read between the lines or try to understand the subtext.
As the play is set in New Orleans, the dramatist describes the place and the atmosphere of the French Quarter and mentions the multiracial and multicultural character of the city before the action of the play begins. He suggests a rather authentic setting of the play when he describes the poor two-storey building which is typical of the houses in the French Quarter. But he also conveys the atmosphere of the place in a poetic way when he writes that "it has a raffish charm" and the sky is "a peculiarly tender blue [...] which invests the scene with a kind of lyricism and gracefully attenuates the atmosphere of decay." (p. 10, ll. 4 f, 9 ff) As the first scene of the play takes place in the evening early in May, Tennessee Williams also mentions the warm breeze, the smells of bananas and coffee, the voices of the people in the street and the jazz music that can be heard everywhere. In particular he underlines that the tinny "'Blue Piano' expresses the spirit of the life which goes on here." (p. 10, ll. 19 f)
In his stage directions Tennessee Williams also informs about the age, the size, the appearance, the social position, the traits and habits of the characters, their movements and emotional behaviour, their way of talking or being silent, their facial play and gestures, etc. Blanche's appearance for in-

stance is described as "incongruous" to the poor setting and her expression as one of "shocked disbelief" (cf. p. 12, ll. 18 f). The dramatist also alludes to her avoiding bright light as one of the recurring characteristics of the protagonist and poetically points out that "there is something about her uncertain manner, as well as her white clothes, that suggests a moth." (p. 12, ll. 23 ff) When she meets her sister "she begins to speak with feverish vivacity as if she feared for either of them to stop and think." (p. 15, ll. 2 f) When she is uncertain whether Stanley will like her, "her voice drops and her look is frightened" (p. 18, ll. 36 f). At the end of the play Blanche "makes a shocked gesture" and "stands quite still for some moments [...] and a look of sorrowful perplexity as though all human experience shows on her face." (p. 102, ll. 17 ff)

The dramatist describes Stanley's and Stella's apartment because it contributes to the conflicts between Stanley and Blanche since Stanley and Stella live in cramped conditions. There are only a kitchen and a bedroom with a bathroom. Blanche is supposed to sleep on a folding bed in the kitchen, where Stanley and his friends are used to play poker until late at night. There is no door between the kitchen and the bedroom but only a portiere. To get into the bathroom they have to pass the bedroom. Thus Tennessee Williams creates a stage that does not allow any privacy. Consequently Blanche feels uneasy and Stanley and Stella are no longer able to continue the life they are used to, in particular their sex life. Stanley considers Blanche as an intruder and rhetorically asks his wife: "And wasn't we happy together, wasn't it all okay till she showed here?" (p. 84, ll. 35 f) When Stella is upset about her husband's rude behaviour on Blanche's birthday and cries, Stanley tries to comfort her: "Stell, it's gonna be all right after she goes and after you've got the baby. It's gonna be all right again between you and me the way it was. You remember that way that it was? Them nights we had together? God, honey, it's gonna be sweet when we can make noise in the night the way that we used to and get the colored lights going with nobody's sister behind the curtains to hear us!" (p. 82, ll. 16 ff) But the curtain also enables Mitch to see Blanche when she changes her clothes and "stands in the light through the portieres" (p. 38, l. 28) and become interested in her. As the bathroom is frequently occupied by Blanche, Stanley gets furious. On the other hand it allows Mitch to meet Blanche on his way there in the bedroom and talk to her the first time. The bedroom serves various purposes. It is for instance the place where the characters change their clothes, Mitch tries to rape Blanche, Stanley rapes her and Blanche flees to when she panics before being taken to the mental hospital.

The stage property Tennessee Williams mentions such as a folding bed, table and chairs, a portiere, a bed, a whisky bottle and a tumbler, Blanche's trunk and clothes, her young husband's love letters, her hand mirror, etc. are necessary for the action and the presentation of Blanche's character and behav-

iour. Contrary to Blanche's white dress and her other extravagant clothes and costume jewellery Tennessee Williams describes the vivid colours of the men's rather tasteless shirts. Van Gogh's painting of a billiard-parlour at night contrasts with the poker scene in Stanley's kitchen (cf. p. 35, ll. 1 ff).
Moreover, the playwright frequently mentions various dramatic and technical devices such as different sound effects. The "blue piano" and sometimes a "hot trumpet" and drums can be heard, which are meant to convey an authentic atmosphere of New Orleans but also emphasize the characters' mood and actions. The characters' behaviour and feelings are frequently characterized by their laughter and shouts. A cat's screech for instance, the tamale vendor's shouts, Stanley's noisy behaviour and an approaching train make Blanche startle and thus stress her nervous state of character. The sound of running water in the bathroom signals that Blanche is taking one of her hot baths again to calm her nerves, which upsets Stanley who also gets furious when Blanche turns on the radio. When Stanley desperately shouts Stella's name, his state of mind is reflected by a moaning low-tone clarinet (cf. p. 45, l. 17) and Blanche's fear is accompanied by the "hectic breakdown" of the distant piano music (cf. p. 79, l. 12). Before Stanley rapes Blanche, honky-tonk music, the noise of a locomotive, inhuman jungle voices and the hot trumpet and drums from a bar are heard and stress an atmosphere of violence. In Scene Seven there is a sharp contrast between Blanche singing in the bathroom and Stanley informing Stella about her sister's life in Laurel. The same applies to Blanche's "dismal birthday supper" and to the "bellowing laughter" upstairs (cf. p. 80, l. 7; p. 82, l. 23).
As Blanche frequently hears the polka tune that was played when she was dancing with Allan the night he shot himself dead, it has a dramatic effect. The so-called Varsouviana is followed by the shot, which signals the end of her being haunted by her guilty conscience. The music and the shot are supposed to be heard only by Blanche – and the audience – whereas the other characters do not hear the sounds and only believe that she is extremely nervous. When Stanley mentions Blanche's marriage in Scene One, "the music of the polka rises up, faint in the distance" (p. 24, l. 6). It thus signals that Blanche is reminded of her late husband's fate again. In Scene Six she tells Mitch about her young husband's suicide and the polka tune changes from a minor to a major key and increases to emphasize her imagining the shocking event until the music fades out when Mitch kisses her. When Mitch has stood her up, Scene Eight and Scene Nine are connected by the Varsouviana "rising with sinister rapidity" (p. 85, l. 10), which expresses Blanche's fright and confusion. She hears "the rapid, feverish polka tune, the 'Varsouviana' [...]. The music is in her mind; she is drinking to escape it and the sense of disaster closing in on her" (p. 86, ll. 4 ff). When she tells Mitch that she hears the polka tune and the shot that generally ends it, he believes that she is mad (cf. p. 87, l. 30). The music fades in again when a blind Mexican woman selling

flowers for the dead appears and Blanche is reminded of her dying relatives at Belle Reve. The tune fades out after the flower vendor disappeared. Finally the polka tune is played softly and distantly in Scene Eleven but is weirdly distorted when Blanche panics before the Doctor takes her to the mental hospital.
The stage setting and the sets need not be changed since all the eleven scenes take place inside the house or in front of it. To indicate a change of place the playwright makes use of lighting. Thus the action starts on the steps of the two-storey building and continues on the street in front of it and on the first landing of the house. But when Eunice opens the door of the downstairs apartment, it is lighted while the surrounding areas dim out. When Stanley goes into the bedroom, and Blanche and Stella meet outside the house, "the inner rooms fade to darkness and the outside wall of the house is visible." (p. 34, ll. 5 f) Thus the dramatist uses a modern stage technique that allows to perform the play without an interruption and the audience can concentrate on the part of the stage where the main action takes place, for instance the kitchen, the bedroom, the area in front of the bathroom, the porch, etc.
Tennessee Williams sometimes combines various effects to mirror Blanche's state of mind and to increase the stage effect, for instance when she feels to be in a trap and tries to ring up Shep Huntleigh in vain: "The night is filled with inhuman voices like cries in a jungle. The shadows and lurid reflections move sinuously as flames along the wall spaces. Through the back wall of the rooms, which have become transparent, can be seen the sidewalk. A prostitute has rolled a drunkard. He pursues her along the walk, overtakes her and there is a struggle. A policeman's whistle breaks it up." (p. 97, ll. 32 ff) Sounds, light effects and the criminal action in the backdrop stress Blanche's confusion, allude to her getting insane and underline her desperate situation in the run-down surroundings of the apartment she desires to leave.
In Scene Eleven her terror is accompanied by "lurid reflections", "a weird distortion" of the polka tune and "the cries and noises of the jungle" (p. 105, ll. 27 ff). But when the Doctor leads her out of the apartment Blanche's subsiding terror corresponds to the light and sound effects since "the lurid reflections fade from the walls, the inhuman cries and noises die out and her own hoarse crying is calmed" (p. 107, ll. 23 ff). When her sister's "luxurious sobbing" and Stanley's "sensual murmur fade away under the swelling music of the 'blue piano' and the muted trumpet" (p. 108, ll. 22 ff), the playwright alludes to the fact that life in the French Quarter seems to go on as it used to be. But the reader or spectator might doubt that it is possible for Stella and Mitch since they are deeply moved by Blanche's tragic fate and their own guilt.

4. The Major Themes and Motifs

In the Foreword to his *Memoirs* (p. xvii) Tennessee Williams points out that he can only write about his own experiences and problems and transmute them into poetry and drama: "My thing is what it always was: to express my world and my experience of it in whatever form seems suitable to the material." And about the characters of his plays he states: "I must find characters that correspond to my own tensions." (Nancy Tischler, p. 246, quoted from: Sambrook, p. 9) Thus some of Blanche's traits such as her sensitivity and fragility together with her insanity and being taken to a mental hospital remind of his sister's character and fate. Stella's guilty conscience corresponds to the dramatist's own life-long guilt-ridden feelings about his sister Rose, whose brain operation he should have prevented as he believed. In his *Memoirs* he refers to Blanche several times and identifies with her, e.g. when he states that "there has always been in me the conviction of Blanche, that 'deliberate cruelty is the one unforgivable thing'" (p. 170; cf. *Streetcar*, p. 96, ll. 24 f) and "I have always depended upon the kindness of strangers" (*Memoirs*, p. 131; cf. *Streetcar*, p. 107, ll. 35 f). "Actually it was true, I always had, and without being often disappointed. In fact, I would guess that chance acquaintances, or strangers, have usually been kinder to me than friends – which does not speak too well for me. To know me is not to love me. At best, it is to tolerate me [...]" (*Memoirs*, p. 131).

Several motifs are taken from his own life. In his *Memoirs* (p. 12) he for instance points out that his ancestors were of French origin and he traces a line of his ancestors back to the Huguenots like Blanche: "We are French by extraction. Our first American ancestors were French Huguenots." (p. 37) Blanche's characterization as a Southern belle reminds of his mother and his own Southern background and love of the South and also nostalgically of the old South represented by Blanche. Like Blanche his sister "lost a beau" when he killed himself (p. 121) and his sister "Rose's passion, as well as Blanche's, was clothes" (p. 120).

Stanley reminds of the dramatist's father who loved poker games, light ladies and alcohol, but also demanded to be honest (cf. *Memoirs*, p. 13). Whereas he asked his son to become a member of the ATO student fraternity, Blanche mentions that she wore the ATO pin of Shep Huntleigh. Like Tennessee Williams she is a heavy smoker and alcoholic and Mitch is also a member of the New Orleans Athletic Club and likes swimming.

But all the biographical elements are transformed into something new, since they are used to create dramatic characters and situations that constitute the imaginative world of a play that differs from Tennessee Williams' life. The fundamental themes, however, he deals with such as love and sex, violence and death, loneliness, hope and despair are of general human relevance and have been turned into plays since the ancient Greek tragedies.

4.1 Desire, love and friendship

The streetcar named Desire really ran in New Orleans and inspired Tennessee Williams to change the former titles of the play such as *The Moth*, *Blanche's Chair in the Moon* and *The Poker Night* into *A Streetcar Named Desire* in order to stress one of the most important themes of the play. This is also achieved at the beginning of the play when Blanche tells that she took a streetcar named Desire. As the word desire means either a very strong wish to have something or the strong wish to have sex with somebody, the two meanings of the word apply to the play.

Stanley for instance does not only have a strong sexual desire but also enjoys good drink and food, games, his car and radio (cf. p. 22, ll. 21 ff). His relationship to his wife is mainly based on sexual desire and Stella has given up the values she has been brought up to to a large extent because she also passionately loves her husband even after being beaten by him. She was thrilled when on their wedding night Stanley smashed all the light bulbs with her slipper. Violence seems to arouse their desire. Blanche calls it "brutal desire" (p. 52, l. 33), which Stanley practises when he rapes Blanche and thus shows that he is the domineering person in his home. Thus Tennessee Williams sometimes links violence and sex, also when he describes the neighbours' relationship. Moreover, sex such as adultery, promiscuity, prostitution, homosexuality and rape is a topic that is frequently alluded to in the play.

Blanche is characterized as sensitive and nervous when she arrives at her sister's home and strongly wishes to find a shelter there and come to peace after the disaster she experienced in Laurel. When she had to take care of her relatives who were fatally ill, she sometimes left the plantation to have sex with the soldiers of a nearby camp and also lived like a prostitute in a hotel in Laurel. When she seduces a seventeen-year-old boy in Laurel and also kisses a young collector of the evening paper in New Orleans, she is obviously driven by desire but also because she cannot forget her seventeen-year-old husband who committed suicide. She tries to make Mitch desire and marry her to find protection and tells him that she had sex with the soldiers in Laurel because she was confronted with death all the time. She believes that the opposite of death is desire (cf. p. 91, l. 20), which makes her feel alive.

Blanche cannot forget her first love: "I loved someone, too, and the person I loved I lost. [...] He was a boy, just a boy, when I was a very young girl. When I was sixteen, I made the discovery – love. All at once and much, much too completely. It was like you suddenly turned a blinding light on something that had always been half in shadow, that's how it struck the world for me." (p. 70, ll. 30 ff) Stella tries to explain her sister's inconsistent and immoral behaviour in Laurel by telling her husband that Blanche was "almost a child" when "she married a boy who wrote poetry. ... He was extremely good-looking. I think Blanche didn't just love him but worshipped the ground he walked on! Adored him and thought him almost too fine to be human!"

(p. 77, ll. 10 ff) But the discovery of his homosexuality "killed her illusions" (p. 77, l. 8). Thus Tennessee Williams seems to underline that Blanche mistook idolatry for love since she was too young to know what true love is. On the other hand she is frequently reminded of her young husband throughout the play when she hears the polka tune and the shot and finally wishes to be dropped after death into "an ocean as blue as [...] my first lover's eyes!" (p. 103, ll. 34 f) Tennessee Williams does not explicitly tell to what extent Blanche really loved her young husband or just imagines loving him. He also seems to leave love a "mystery" since he does not draw a clear line between sexual desire, passionate love and "true" love.

He does not only underline that the characters are driven by sexual desire or passionate "love". He describes Mitch's love of his mother and also employs the word "love" when Stella describes her feelings for her husband. When Blanche asks her sister to describe Stanley, Stella replies: "Oh, you can't describe someone you're in love with!" (p. 19, l. 10) though her relationship with her husband is mainly based on sex. When Blanche tells Stella that her relationship to her husband is only "brutal desire" and calls it a "devil", Stella repeats that she loves Stanley (cf. p. 53, l. 7). She also accepts Stanley's hot-tempered character, for instance when he smashes things or even beats her when he is furious or drunk, because afterwards he is always tender and kind to her. But she does not have anything else in common with Stanley. At the end of the play neither Stella nor Stanley express that they are happy about their child and love him. Stanley is only proud of having a son and Stella does not show her feelings when Eunice places the baby in her arms. She is only distressed because of her sister's fate she feels responsible of.

Stanley is the incarnation of desire and sex. Tennessee Williams mentions that "since earliest manhood the center of his life has been pleasure with women" and describes him as a "gaudy seed-bearer" (p. 22, ll. 22 f, l. 30). When he caresses his wife or shouts for her, he is mainly driven by sexual desire. He believes to have Stella brought down to his level (cf. p. 84, ll. 33 f) and does not make a difference between sex and love.

Stanley calls Mitch his "buddy" but is unable to be a true friend since he dominates him and the other poker players and does not tolerate them if they do not behave as he wishes them to do. Though he is honest to Mitch when he tells him the truth about Blanche's life in Laurel, Mitch finally attacks him because he has destroyed the magic image of Blanche he was fascinated by to such an extent that he wished to marry her to overcome his loneliness.

Tennessee Williams presents characters that do not really differentiate between love and sex. They seem to be unable to feel true love but are mainly driven by sexual desire, which reminds of the symbolic title of the play. But the playwright also shows that it is possible to feel love or to realize that sex and love can belong together. The word "desire" is mainly used in the sense

of sexual desire but Blanche and Mitch seem to long for true love they are unable to realize because of Blanche's promiscuous past and Mitch's inability to understand and accept her as she is.
Also true friendship seems to be impossible since Stanley and his poker players including Mitch do not share each other's problems. The characters do not really tolerate each other and do not accept each other as he or she is since they see each other mainly from their own point of view.
But possibly Tennessee Williams indirectly (in the subtext) alludes to man's final destination, which is understanding and true love.

4.2 Loneliness and the lack of understanding

In his *Memoirs* (p. 99) Tennessee Williams states that his "greatest affliction, which is perhaps the major theme of my writings" is "the affliction of loneliness that follows me like a shadow [...]."
In *A Streetcar Named Desire* Blanche is looking for protection since she feels lonely. Her young husband committed suicide and her sister left her alone on the plantation where her other relatives died one after the other. She tried to overcome her loneliness by several affairs but was only abused by her lovers.
Stanley mistrusts Blanche from the very beginning of the play and wants her to leave his home because Blanche makes his intimate life with his wife impossible. Stella also decides to get rid of her sister, when she finally deceives her and arranges her being taken to a mental hospital.
Blanche tries to make Mitch desire her since she realizes that "people don't see you – *men* don't – don't even admit your existence unless they are making love to you. And you've got to have your existence admitted by someone, if you're going to have someone's protection." (p. 58, ll. 29 ff) When she tells Mitch that he will be lonely after his mother's death and honestly describes her young husband's death, Mitch draws her into his arms saying: "You need somebody. And I need somebody, too. Could it be – you and me, Blanche?" She sobs and replies: "Sometimes – there's God – so quickly!" (p. 72, ll. 3 ff) Thus for a short time true communication seems to be possible. But when Mitch is informed about her immoral life at Laurel, he refuses to marry her because his mother would not accept her as his wife. He leaves her alone though Blanche honestly tells him the truth. At the end of the play he seems to regret the loss of Blanche. He is depressed and feels lonely again whereas Blanche seems to retain her dignity when she leaves the stage. But in fact she is deceived and is going to live the lonely life of mentally sick people. Thus Blanche is abandoned by everybody she knows and seems to personify human loneliness.
Throughout the play Tennessee Williams stresses the inability of his characters to understand each other really. Though Stella tries to be kind to Blanche and even supports her sister's vanity by asking her husband and Eunice to

admire Blanche's outward appearance and by hiding her sister's true age, she does not feel guilty of having left her alone at Belle Reve and finally betrays her when she needs her help most. Stanley is only interested in knowing the truth about the loss of the plantation and Blanche's life in Laurel. He is unable to flatter her and understand her behaviour and mental problems. Even when she tells the truth to Mitch, her "beau" is unable to understand her desperate situation and accept her as she is.

Blanche herself contributes to her being misunderstood and left alone because she is unable to tolerate Stanley's way of life though she once tells Stella: "But maybe he's what we need to mix with our blood now that we've lost Belle Reve and have to go on without Belle Reve to protect us ..." (p. 34, ll. 21 ff). Instead she frequently insults him, tells lies and even tries to deceive Mitch to desire and marry her. She neither overcomes her conceitedness nor her self-deceit when she hopes to be helped by Shep Huntleigh who seems to exist only in her mind. Her several attempts at writing a letter to him or ringing him up fail and appear to be unrealistic. When she is taken to the mental institution at the end of the play she is as helpless and lonely like her young husband who committed suicide because Blanche was unable to understand and help him.

When Blanche leaves the stage at the end of the play, her final words are: "I have always depended on the kindness of strangers." She is not aware of being deceived again as she always was. Moreover, Tennessee Williams seems to allude to the fact that everybody is everybody's stranger and terribly lonely.

4.3 Reality versus imagination

Blanche is unable and unwilling to accept reality as it is. She is shocked by her sister's home and living together with a husband who is "common" and rude. She sticks to the conventional rules of behaviour she was brought up to though she also violates them when she behaves like a prostitute in Laurel. Nevertheless she expects to be treated respectfully. She calls Shep Huntleigh a gentleman and believes that Mitch's and the Doctor's behaviour is gentlemanlike.

Blanche tries to hide the truth and tells lies unless she feels forced or obliged to be honest to win Stella's or Mitch's compassion. She wants to appear beautiful and be admired and therefore puts on fanciful clothes and costume jewellery, which are supposed to hide her fading beauty. When Stanley wants to know the facts about the loss of Belle Reve and wants Blanche to lay "her cards on the table", she replies: "Well, life is too full of evasions and ambiguities" (p. 30, ll. 25 ff) and thus seems to allude also to her own attempts at deluding and deceiving others.

She sometimes behaves like a young girl, which is underlined by the songs she is singing in the bathroom (cf. p. 26, l. 5; p. 74, ll. 21 ff) or when she calls

herself a girl and Mitch and his friends "boys" (cf. p. 88, l. 8). But by the songs she sings Tennessee Williams also alludes to Blanche's situation and dreams. The first song "From the Land of the Sky-blue Water, / They brought a captive maid" expresses Blanche's feeling that she has been taken from Belle Reve to Stanley's home where she is held captive. The second song she sings in the bathroom contrasts with reality. While Stanley informs his wife about her sister's promiscuous life in Laurel, Blanche's song expresses her wish of being loved by Mitch if she could make him believe in her and her dream world though it is based on deceit and self-deceit.
As Blanche is unable to accept her true age and her getting older, she also evades bright light until Mitch tears the paper lantern off the light bulb. She feels insulted by Mitch's wish to see her real face. Contrary to Mitch who wants to be "realistic", Blanche replies: "I don't want realism. [...] I'll tell you what I want. Magic! [...] Yes, yes, magic! I try to give that to people. I misrepresent things to them. I don't tell truth, I tell what *ought* to be truth." (p. 89, ll. 12 ff)

Tennessee Williams thus describes reality as based on facts but also seems to allude to a second form of reality that exists in a person's mind and is based on imagination, illusions and dreams of a better world. While Stanley informs his wife about Blanche's real life in Laurel, Blanche is singing a popular song in the bathroom that expresses her fondness of illusion: "Say, it's only a paper moon, / Sailing over a cardboard sea – But it wouldn't be make-believe If you believed in me!" (p. 74, ll. 21 ff). It also seems to be wishful thinking when she tells that "physical beauty is passing. A transitory possession. But beauty of the mind and richness of the spirit and tenderness of the heart – and I have all of those things – aren't taken away, but grow! Increase with the years!" (p. 96. ll. 6 ff)
The more Blanche is frightened and panics the more she lives in a dream world. She frantically tries to ring up Shep Huntleigh and believes that this millionaire, who seems to exist only in her mind, will take her on a Caribbean cruise and thus rescue her. She loses her sense of reality and seems to become insane. She mixes up former experiences and impressions when she describes her death on the sea. At the end of the play she is no longer able to recognize her real situation but believes that the Doctor helps her to get out of the trap of Stanley's home. Blanche is not able or willing to adapt to the way of life in the French Quarter like her sister but maintains the facade of a Southern belle and flees into her dream world but in reality is taken to a lunatic asylum.

Marlon Brando as Stanley and Vivien Leigh as Blanche in Elia Kazan's film (1951)

4.4 Violence and softness

Tennessee Williams frequently deals with the topic of physical violence in his plays. In *A Streetcar Named Desire* Stanley seems to be the incarnation of violence since he is hot-tempered and aggressive, in particular when he is drunk. He dominates his wife and commands his poker friends. When Stella asks him to clear the table, he smashes the dishes and he hurls everything from the poker table that in his opinion should not lie there. He violently opens Blanche's trunk, throws her clothes to the floor and snatches her love letters without caring for her feelings. When Blanche wants to listen to the radio he throws it out of the window. He even beats his pregnant wife when she criticizes him. Throughout the play he treats Blanche without understanding her desperate situation or sharing her troubles. Instead he treats her relentlessly and finally rapes her.

There are several other examples of physical violence in the play, for instance the row of Eunice and Steve, the poker friends' struggling with Stanley, Mitch's attempt at raping Blanche and the struggle of a prostitute and a drunkard who was robbed by her. Even Blanche smashes her hand-mirror violently down and threatens to thrust the top of a broken bottle in Stanley's face before she is raped by him. At the end of the play Stanley pushes Mitch aside who accuses Stanley of being responsible of Blanche's fate, Mitch hits Stanley and even wants to kill him and Blanche "turns wildly and scratches at the Matron" (p. 107, ll. 14 f) when the nurse tries to prevent her flight and also wants to put Blanche into a straitjacket. Violence can also be directed

against oneself, e.g. when Allan Grey commits suicide, which Blanche describes in an extremely brutal way: "He'd stuck the revolver into his mouth, and fired – so that the back of his head had been – blown away!" (p. 71, ll. 31 ff)
But violence is also used in form of psychological cruelty, e.g. when Blanche accuses her sister of having left her alone at Belle Reve to be "in bed with your – Polack", which makes Stella cry and leave for the bathroom (cf. p. 21, l. 26). Mitch, who is at first friendly and polite, treats Blanche cruelly after being informed about her past and does not care for her desperate situation but even tries to rape her.
But though Stanley reacts violently when he is drunk, feels insulted or believes that anybody does not respect his domineering role, he becomes soft and tender when he is sober again after having beaten his wife. He caresses her at the end of the play when he tries to comfort Stella in his way after Blanche has been taken to the mental hospital. Thus Tennessee Williams presents mixed characters with contradictory traits. They do not remain what they appear to be at first sight.
In an essay of 1959 Tennessee Williams justifies his writing about "violence in American life only because I am not so well acquainted with the society of other countries." (*Essays*, p. 108) In an interview of 1960 he states:

> "In our lives violence, not physical violence but emotional violence, is so much a part of us. I have seen so much depicted of people's longing to meet each other tenderly with love, and violence is represented because it's the obstacle, it's the other side of the coin, it's the dark side of the moon, however you want to put it, but the dark side of the moon is in the sky and we want to show both sides of the moon you know." (*Conversations*, p. 77)

4.5 Disease and death

In his *Memoirs* Tennessee Williams describes his own long disease when he was a child, his mother's hysteria and his sister's insanity, his father's and his own alcoholism, his eye cataract, nervous breakdowns, addiction to drugs and fear of dying from cancer. Physical and mental disease accompanied him as long as he lived. His lover Frank died from cancer and his favourite poet Hart Crane committed suicide. Thus the dramatist frequently deals with the topics of disease and death in his plays.
In *A Streetcar Named Desire* Blanche takes care of her mortally sick relatives, loses her young husband who commits suicide and finally gets mentally deranged herself. Stella only returns to Belle Reve for the funerals. Blanche stresses the horror of sickness and dying she felt when she was left alone on the plantation: "I, I, *I* took the blows in my face and my body! All of those deaths! The long parade to the graveyard! Father, mother! Margaret, that

dreadful way! So big with it, it couldn't be put in a coffin! But had to be burned like rubbish! [...] Funerals are quiet, but deaths – not always. Sometimes their breathing is hoarse, and sometimes it rattles, and sometimes they even cry out to you, 'Don't let me go!' Even the old, sometimes, say, 'Don't let me go.'" (p. 21, ll. 1 ff)

Similar to Blanche, who lost her young husband, Mitch's girl-friend died young. Like Blanche he takes care of his mortally sick mother but is finally unable to marry Blanche though she honestly tells him about her life at Belle Reve. When a blind Mexican woman is passing in front of the house selling tin flowers and wreaths for funerals, Blanche is again reminded of her dying relatives at Belle Reve and utters fragments of her shocking experiences such as "blood-stained pillow-slips" and "Death – I used to sit here and she used to sit over there and death was as close as you are. ... We didn't dare even admit we had ever heard of it!" (p. 91, ll. 11 f; ll. 16 ff) She tries to overcome her horror of death and desires to begin a new life with Mitch, who seems to understand her because he is the only character in the play apart from Blanche who takes death seriously since his first love died and his mother is mortally sick. Though also Stella lost her relatives, she did not care much as it seems but only went to their funerals and enjoys her sex life with Stanley. But when she is unable to go on listening to her sister's shocking and insulting words, she starts crying.

While playing poker Stanley is bragging that he survived the war when four out of five comrades lost their lives at Salerno where his corps landed. But he neither shows compassion with the comrades he lost in the war nor with Mitch's sorrows because of his mortally sick mother. He is not willing or unable to understand his "buddy" but hurts his feelings (cf. p. 36, ll. 4 ff).

Blanche's insanity at the end of the play is already alluded to in Scene One when she admits "I was so exhausted by all I'd been through my – nerves broke. [...] I was on the verge of – lunacy, almost!" (p. 16, ll. 32 ff) Before she is taken to the mental hospital, she is frequently characterized as being nervous, hysterical, frightened, panicking, "boxed out of her mind" (p. 87, l. 30) and having illusions such as being rescued by Shep Huntleigh or being on a ship and wishing to die with her "hand in the hand of some nice-looking ship's doctor" and be "sewn up in a clean white sack and dropped overboard – at noon – in the blaze of summer – and into an ocean as blue as [...] my first lover's eyes!" (p. 103, ll. 28 ff) Her stay in the mental hospital for the rest of her life may be understood as being buried alive.

As Blanche is unable to give up her views and values of the Old South and adapt to the new way of life like her sister, she is an outsider. The more so as she is unable to cope with her sexual desire, the decadence of her ancestors, the corruption of the old values, her guilt, her own immoral life in Laurel, her destitute and helpless situation. Without any hope she despairs and gets insane since nobody is able to understand her contradictory views and behaviour. Instead of facing reality she flees into a dream world. Contrary to Stanley who seems to represent the new American way of life Blanche is unfit for the "rat race" of survival in the modern society. Eunice finally underlines that there is no other place for her to go but the lunatic asylum (cf. p. 106, ll. 35 f). When Tennessee Williams was asked "why writers are so preoccupied with disease and death", he answered: "Any artist dies two deaths, [...] not only his own as a physical being but that of his creative power, it dies with him." (*Memoirs*, pp. 241 f)

4.6 Gender roles, moral values and religion

Gender roles

At first sight Tennessee Williams seems to distinguish between the social roles of men and women rather strictly since Stanley is characterized as strongly built, proud and powerful. He dominates his wife who stays at home and has to clean the apartment, prepare the meals, decorate and clear the table and is forbidden to give orders to him. He earns and controls the money, pays the bills and irregularly gives her some pocket-money. Stella seems to accept her husband's domineering role since she lives in a society that is dominated by men. Stanley behaves like a macho and is loud, aggressive and intolerant. Also his friends seem to be characterized in a stereotype way when they enjoy sex, dirty jokes, gambling, bowling, playing poker and drinking beer.

Stella, however, is characterized as a mild and understanding woman who tries to find a compromise between her husband and her sister. She also tolerates her husband's pleasures such as playing poker or bowling. She accepts it that those are pass time activities only for men. Stanley allows his wife to watch him bowling but denies Blanche to "kibitz" when he plays poker and Mitch exclaims that poker should not be played in front of women. As women's pleasures Stella mentions going to the movies and playing bridge. Stella cries after being accused by her sister and Blanche is sobbing several times, which seems to underline that women do not hide their feelings but tend to shed tears when they are sad.

But despite such stereotype gender roles Tennessee Williams does not reinforce them since Stella also insults her husband because of his table manners and criticizes his behaviour towards her sister. She accuses him of being cruel to Blanche and even states: "Nobody, nobody, was tender and trusting as she was. But people like you abused her, and forced her to change." (p. 84, ll. 19 ff) But though Stanley beats her and she flees to her neighbour, she returns to him because she is driven by desire. Also Eunice does not totally obey her husband but starts a row and beats and hurts him. She orders him to come home in time for lunch and if he does not, he is told to buy and eat a cheap sandwich.

Though Stanley beats his wife when he is drunk, "he breaks into sobs" (p. 44, l. 27) and shouts for Stella after she has left him. He treats Blanche rudely and wants to get rid of her, but becomes soft and caresses his despairing wife after Blanche has left for the mental hospital.

Tennessee Williams also does not generalize characteristics such as kindness, tenderness, softness and compassion as typically female traits of character. Mitch for instance is also characterized by his love and taking care of his mortally sick mother, his tenderness towards Blanche when she feels lonely and his collapsing and sobbing when Blanche is taken to the mental institution and Stanley calls him a "cry-baby" (p. 107. l. 9). Blanche's young husband is characterized by Stella as a boy who wrote poems and was soft and kind. When Blanche tells Mitch that "there was something different about the boy, a nervousness, a softness and tenderness which wasn't like a man's, although he wasn't the least bit effeminate looking" (p. 70, l. 38 – p. 71, l. 1), Tennessee Williams also seems to allude to his own homosexuality.

Though the gender relations seem to be mainly based on mutual desire and sex and both men and women can be promiscuous, Blanche explains her "many intimacies with strangers" with her "hunting for some protection" (cf. p. 90, ll. 8 ff). Blanche believes in the conventional role of man as the protector of his wife and women's dependence on men. Consequently she wishes to marry for protection and therefore tries to seduce and deceive Mitch by making use of so-called female qualities such as beauty, friendliness, imagination but also lies and tears. She wants to appear attractive and be flattered and therefore puts on various dresses, jewellery and perfume. She hides her true age because Mitch is younger than she is and she fears that he would not marry her since wives are – as she believes – conventionally younger than their husbands and men are not interested in girls over thirty (cf. p. 60, ll. 13 f). Due to the gender role she believes to have no choice but to conceal her promiscuous life in Laurel and knows that "men don't want anything they get too easy" (p. 60, ll. 11 f).

She also believes that "the lady must entertain the gentleman" (p. 60, ll. 30 f) and repeatedly demands that men should behave like gentlemen as if the conventions of the Old South were still practised. But at the end of the play she is deceived by the Doctor who makes her believe that he is a gentleman when he treats her kindly. The Matron, however, appears to have traditionally male traits of character since she is strongly built, rude and forces Blanche down.

Despite her conventional views of gender roles Blanche also seems to have a glimpse of women's emancipation when she urges Stella to leave her husband and to establish a shop with her to be independent. But as they do not have enough money to realize her idea and need the financial support of Shep Huntleigh, who to a large extent seems to be an imaginary figure, Blanche's suggestion is illusionary. She also does not recognize Stella's strong affection for Stanley. When she claims to be socially and intellectually superior to others because of her aristocratic ancestors and her education, she does not recognize that in Stanley's world such qualities do not count to be accepted and respected. On the contrary, Stanley proves his superiority over her by being realistic and violent.

Moral values

Blanche loved and adored her young husband but when she discovered that he was gay, she did not help him but was the reason of his suicide, which does not only remind of Hart Crane's fate but also alludes to the laws and prejudices against homosexuals in America at Tennessee Williams' times when homosexuality was considered immoral and a criminal offence in various American states. On the one hand Blanche has internalized the conventional view of homosexuality but on the other hand she feels guilty of having denied any understanding and help. She criticizes her ancestors' promiscuity but lives in the same way before she loses her job in Laurel. She kisses the paper collector though she knows that it is not morally acceptable.
"Tennessee Williams has repeatedly affirmed being a moralist. Asked whether he writes with an ethical purpose, he answered: 'Yes, definitely, intensively so.'" (Ingrid Rogers, p. 1) In his *Memoirs* (pp. 230 f) he demands "a New Morality" and seems to allude to the loss of understanding and compassion in modern America. Referring to Blanche he states that "nearly all of her cries to the world in her season of desperation have survived because they were true cries of her embattled heart; that is what gave them the truth which has made them live on, echoing in the hearts of so many known and unknown ladies."
Several moral values such as honesty, the love of truth, decency, helping diseased and weak people, being kind and sympathetic to others are frequently violated by the characters in the play but also practised to a certain extent.
Blanche for instance takes care of her sick relatives contrary to her sister Stella. But at the same time she behaves indecently in Laurel when she is promiscuous. The school authority and the mayor of the town who also represent law, order and moral standards dismiss her and order her to leave Laurel. They do not consider her desperate situation after the death of her relatives and the loss of Belle Reve. Blanche knows that she has to stick to social rules, conventions and moral values. But her desire and her memory of her beloved young husband are stronger, e.g. when she says: "I've got to keep hold of myself" after having drunk whisky (cf. p. 14, l. 32) or after kissing the young collector: "I've got to be good – and keep my hands off children" (p. 62, l. 39). Blanche tells lies to be accepted by others and find protection. She is aware of her deceits and believes that "life is too full of evasions and ambiguities". When Stanley wants her to tell the truth about the loss of Belle Reve, she no longer wants to make use of "double-talk" (p. 31, l. 14). But nevertheless she continues to tell lies as long as she believes that they might help her. How-

ever, she begins to tell the truth as soon as she feels that it is more helpful, e.g. to arouse Mitch's compassion and make him wish to marry her (cf. p. 70, l. 30 – p. 72, l. 11).
As Stanley is unable and unwilling to understand Blanche's emotions and lies, he contributes to her despair and mental decline when he insists on knowing the truth about her and the loss of Belle Reve. He thus follows the social and moral values of justice and truth, since according to the Napoleonic Code he has the right to own what his wife owns and does not want to be cheated and deceived by Blanche. At the same time he is selfish and greedy because neither Stella nor he himself did anything to rescue the plantation. Thus Tennessee Williams makes aware of the fact that social and moral values can also be misused and destroy people. But also following moral values can be harmful since Stanley feels responsible for his friend Mitch and warns him of marrying Blanche, which causes her despair and contributes to her feeling lost and becoming insane.
Though Blanche violates the value of decent behaviour in Laurel, she demands good manners, politeness, gentlemanlike behaviour and gallantry from Stanley and Mitch. As her brother-in-law is unable to behave as she wishes, she deeply offends him. As she wants to marry Mitch to find a safe place where she could live, she tries to seduce and deceive him. She pretends to stick to "old-fashioned ideals" (p. 68, l. 22) when he wants to caress her and she rejects him. Mitch respects her and treats her politely as long as he does not know anything about her indecent life in Laurel. But when he learns the truth about her, he tries to rape her.
Stanley, who appears to be honest and realistic and is not willing to be deluded by Blanche's lies and her hypocrisies, behaves hypocritically himself when he overhears her talk with Stella at the end of the fourth scene but behaves as if he did not listen when he enters the apartment. Even Stella, who first treats her sister in a kind and sympathetic way, deceives her because she "tried to gloss things over a little" in her letters (p. 26, l. 9). When she arranges that Blanche is taken to a mental hospital at the end of the play, she feels that her deceit is unacceptable. She is even criticized by her neighbour Steve: "This is no way to do it. She should've been told." (p. 107, l. 1) Moreover, Stella deceives herself because she is not willing to believe that her husband raped her sister. Since Stanley keeps Blanche's rape a secret and Stella does not tell him that she knows about it, their future family life will be based on a grand delusion.
Whereas the poker players do not react in the Poker Scene when Blanche enters and asks them to remain sitting (cf. p. 37, l. 8), they "stand back" (p. 108, l. 1) when she is led out of the apartment at the end of the play as if they feel that Blanche has been ill-treated and deserves their respect.
Tennessee Williams shows that none of the characters of his play is only bad or good. All of them more or less violate social and moral values. It seems as

if Blanche is right when she comments on the chime of the cathedral bells: "Those cathedral bells – they're the only clean thing in the Quarter." (p. 103, ll. 14 f) But Tennessee Williams underlines in a letter of 1950 that *A Streetcar Named Desire* is "an extremely and peculiarly moral play, in the deepest and truest sense of the term. [...] It is a poetic plea for comprehension." (*Selected Letters*, p. 355)

Religion

Tennessee Williams states in his *Memoirs* (p. 23) that he believes in God, and he also confesses that he has always prayed to God on his knees "when a situation in which I found myself (and there have been many) seemed critical enough in my opinion to merit the Lord's attention and, I trust, intervention." In *A Streetcar Named Desire* he mentions God several times.
When Mitch embraces Blanche and alludes to marrying her, Blanche is deeply moved and grateful since she believes to have found love and security and says: "Sometimes – there's God – so quickly!" (p. 72, l. 11) Stella despairs when her sister leaves for the mental hospital and expresses her deeply felt remorse by repeating the name of God three times and finally exclaims: "Oh, God, what have I done to my sister?" (p. 106, ll. 26 ff) Even Pablo exclaims in Spanish: "Madre de Dios!" when Blanche is so badly treated (cf. p. 107, l. 2).
Blanche frequently takes a bath as if to purify herself from the sin of having ignored her young husband's need for help. She also wants to put on a Della Robbia blue jacket before she leaves Stella's home. As it is "the blue of the robe in the old Madonna pictures" (p. 103, ll 4 f) she seems to allude to her wish of being innocent and rescued.
So all of them, also Stanley, are mixed characters with positive and negative traits. The main reason of their behaviour is not that they are evil but that they are unable or unwilling to understand each other as they are. In a letter to Elia Kazan, the director of the stage production of *A Streetcar Named Desire*, Tennessee Williams writes: "There are no 'good' or 'bad' people. Some are a little better or a little worse but all are activated more by misunderstanding than malice." (Williams, *Letters*, Vol. II, p. 95; cf. "Additional Materials", IV,1)

5. Form and Structure of the Play

Modern tragedy

A Streetcar Named Desire is a modern tragedy since the protagonist is doomed to fail because she is caught in the web of her own lies and illusions and is unable to find protection and peace since she is misunderstood by others and abused by men and finally destroyed by Stanley's determination to reveal the

truth about her indecent life in Laurel and by raping her. When Blanche has lost Belle Reve, is fired and ordered to leave the town, she is destitute and helpless. The only place where she hopes to find refuge is her sister's home. But her last resort develops into a trap where she is raped by her brother-in-law and deceived by her sister. Her final destination, a mental hospital, seems to be a kind of cemetery where she is buried alive, which Tennessee Williams foreshadows when at the beginning of the play Blanche changes the streetcar called Desire for the streetcar running to the final stop Cemetery. Also the street where Stanley and Stella live, Elysian Fields, alludes to death, since in Greek mythology it is the home of the dead in the underworld. Tennessee Williams makes use of tragic irony when Blanche hopes to find protection in her sister's home and tells Mitch: "There was nowhere else I could go." (p. 90, l. 19) Eunice uses nearly the same words at the end of the play when Blanche is going to be taken to the mental hospital: "She couldn't stay here; there wasn't no other place for her to go." (p. 106, ll. 35 f)
Thus Blanche is already in a hopeless situation at the very beginning of the play which is revealed in the following scenes until she is no longer able to distinguish between reality and illusion. She is left alone by everybody and finally deluded into believing that she is led out of a trap and going to find protection. Since the audience or the readers together with Stanley, Stella and Mitch get to know Blanche's past step by step, the play is an analytical drama, which ends with the total failure and destruction of the protagonist. Also Mitch and Stella seem to be in a tragic conflict to a certain extent. Mitch has to decide whether to marry Blanche despite her indecent past or to leave her and Stella has to decide whether to support her sister and leave her husband or to deceive her and stay with her family. Since Mitch even tries to rape Blanche and Stella finally makes her sister believe that she will go on holiday, they contribute to Blanche's increasing insanity. Their remorse and despair at the end of the play seem rather melodramatic but are supposed to make the audience or the reader reflect on Blanche's tragic fate and on the question to what extent Blanche has changed Stella's and Mitch's attitude towards life. Stanley, however, seems to be only content with having saved his home from Blanche as an intruder who endangered his way of life.

Formally seen, the play is not divided into acts but consists of eleven scenes, which can be performed without any interruptions, breaks or curtains. Tennessee Williams admired the ancient Greek theatre (cf. *Essays*, pp. 50 f) and referring to his play *Cat on a Hot Tin Roof* he states: "It adheres to the valuable edict of Aristotle that a tragedy must have unity of time and place and magnitude of theme." (*Memoirs*, p. 168) This also applies to *A Streetcar Named Desire* to a certain extent. As the action concentrates on Blanche's fate, Tennessee Williams obviously sticks to the Aristotelian unity of action. Also the subplots such as the poker scenes and the episode of the young collector

The Structure of the Play

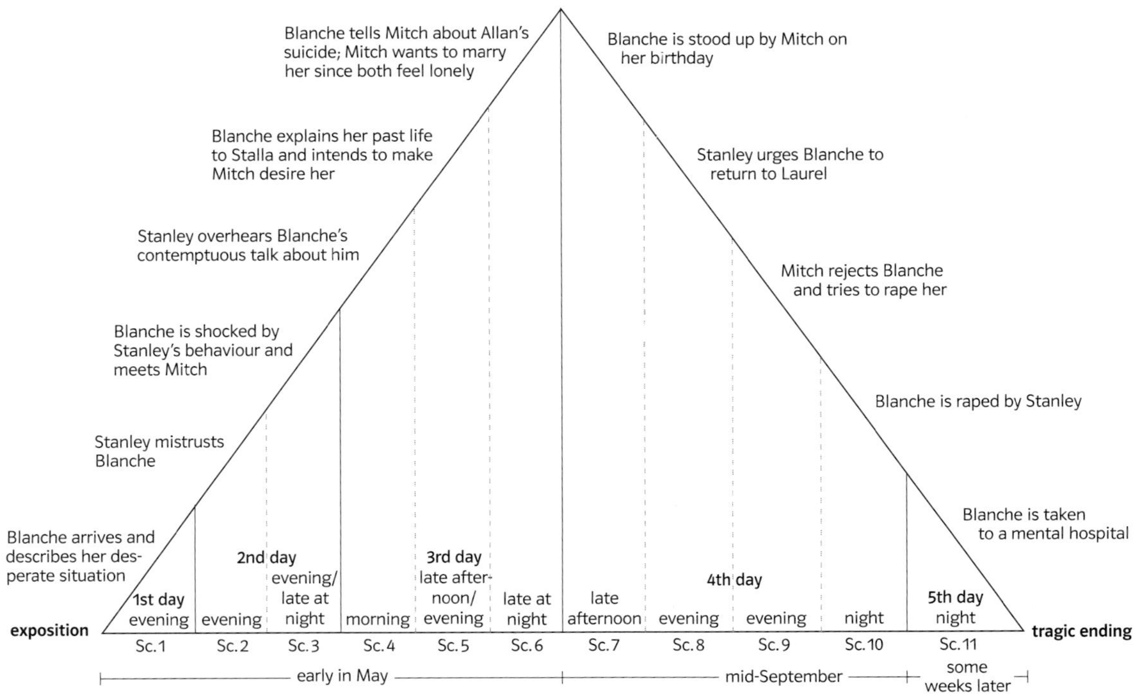

contrast with her way of life or underline it. As there is no change of place, but all the eleven scenes take place near or in the house, the playwright sticks to the unity of place, which Aristotle did not insist on but was ascribed to him by Renaissance literary critics. According to Aristotle's description of the ancient tragedy the unity of time is one day during which the action takes place. But this unity has rarely been practised. Also Tennessee Williams recognized that the unity of time was artificial and impractical but nevertheless made use of the "unity of time" somehow within the play since the second and third scene take place in the same evening, the following three scenes last from morning to late at night of the same day and the seventh to tenth scenes cover the fourth day from late afternoon to the night. The last scene takes place on the fifth day after several weeks.
As Tennessee Williams likes to use dramatic and stylistic devices ambiguously or in a symbolic way, most of the scenes take place in the evening or at night, for instance to stress the atmosphere of Stanley's and his friends' poker parties and Blanche's fear of bright light (cf. Chapter III,4.9).

Tennessee Williams does not subdivide *A Streetcar Named Desire* into the five acts of classical plays or three acts of many modern plays but into eleven scenes that follow one another in chronological order. The action is concentrated on about five days, which reminds of the five acts of classical dramas. The first six scenes play on three days early in May and the following four scenes on one day in mid-September. The last scene plays some weeks later as an aftermath of the tenth scene presenting Blanche's final struggle for protection and deceit by her sister. Thus the play falls into two groups of scenes, which are followed by one final scene. Though three months have passed before the seventh scene begins, there is no indication of an interval which would be possible. Obviously the dramatist intended the play to be performed without any interruption to maintain the audience's attention and suspense.
In the first group of scenes the playwright establishes the major characters, Blanche's desperate situation, her confrontation with Stanley and her meeting Mitch, who seems to fulfil her dream of finding protection. The traditional motif of marriage seems to indicate a happy ending. But since Blanche's rising hope is replaced by her increasing despair in the following scenes, her being stood up by Mitch at her birthday indicates the turning point of the play from a "tragicomedy" to a tragedy. In comparison with the first six scenes the action accelerates in the following four scenes. They present the end of Blanche's dream of marrying Mitch, her futile attempt at winning Mitch by being honest to him and her being raped by Stanley, which can be considered the climax of the play since Blanche becomes the victim of violence and sexual desire, which are the major motifs that cause her physical defeat and mental breakdown. The last scene presents Blanche as a confused

and nearly insane woman who tries to stick to her dream of being rescued. She panics when the Matron tries to force her down. But finally she is deceived by the Doctor's gentlemanlike behaviour and seems to have faith in her future though she is taken to a mental hospital. But as the poker players stand back when Blanche passes them and leaves the stage without turning, she appears to have preserved her human dignity.

As Stanley and Stella seem to continue their way of life they lived before Blanche's arrival, which is stressed by Stanley caressing her, the "swelling music of the 'blue piano' and the muted trumpet" and the fact that the poker play goes on, the play seems to have a circular structure. Blanche's stay was only an intermezzo in the other characters' life in the Vieux Carré. The audience and the readers of the play, however, could continue to reflect on Blanche's life and whether she was destroyed by others or/and herself.

But also the single scenes or the subsequent scenes are structured according to the principles of controversy, conflict, argument and contrast to increase suspense: In the first scene Blanche accuses her sister of having left her alone at Belle Reve and the confrontation between her and Stanley is hinted at. The second scene first centres round the controversy between Stanley and Stella about the loss of Belle Reve and then between Stanley and Blanche. The poker play contrasts with the first meeting of Blanche and Mitch in the third scene. In the fourth scene follows the controversy between Blanche and Stella about leaving Stanley. The fifth scene presents the comic conflict between Stella's neighbours, which contrasts with the serious controversy of Stella and her husband and the conflict between Blanche and Stanley. Stanley's investigations about Blanche foreshadow the information he gives Stella in Scene Seven. The sixth scene which seems to finish with a happy ending of Blanche's and Mitch's relationship is followed by her being stood up by Mitch at her birthday. In Scene Seven Blanche's romantic song contrasts with the truth about her past life told by Stanley, which Stella refuses to believe. In the eighth scene follows the confrontation between Stella and Stanley about his cynical birthday present and in the ninth scene the confrontation between Mitch and Blanche. Scene Ten presents Blanche's and Stanley's final confrontation and her rape. In Scene Eleven the play ends with contrasting the poker play with Blanche's fate, the discrepancy between Blanche's dream world and reality, her resistance against being deceived and Stella's inner conflict.

Before *A Streetcar Named Desire* was produced on Broadway Tennessee Williams mentions Aristotle's idea of *catharsis* (the release of strong feelings through the effect of tragedy) in a letter of April 19, 1947 to Elia Kazan, the stage director of the play: "I remember you asked me what should an audience feel for Blanche. Certainly pity. It is a tragedy with the classic aim of producing a katharsis of pity and terror, and in order to do that Blanche must finally have the understanding and compassion of the audience." (*Letters*, Vol. II, p. 96)

He also refers to Aristotle's idea of *catharsis* when he justifies his writing about violence in the United States in his foreword to the Broadway Opening of his play *Sweet Bird of Youth* (*New York Times*, 8 March 1959; cf. *Essays*, pp. 109 f): "[...] if there is any truth in the Aristotelian idea that violence is purged by its poetic representation on a stage, then it may be that my cycle of violent plays have had a moral justification after all. I know that I have felt it. I have always felt a release from the sense of meaninglessness and death when a work of tragic intention has seemed to me to have achieved that intention, even if only approximately, nearly."

6. Dramatic and Cinematic Devices and Techniques

Tennessee Williams makes use of various dramatic devices which frequently remind of his writing film scripts in Hollywood, e.g. the use of lighting to focus the viewers' attention on a particular section of the stage and the action that takes place there. The beginning of the first scene reminds of an establishing shot since the whole place of action is shown. The dramatist also employs cinematic techniques such as fading in or out, e.g. "the rooms dim out to darkness and the outer walls appear in the night light." (p. 44, ll. 33 f). When Blanche is afraid of being alone in the apartment with Stanley, the back wall becomes transparent and the struggle of a prostitute and a drunkard can be seen. Moreover, the dramatist uses low-key lighting and bright light and several sound effects such as background music to convey the atmosphere of New Orleans. The noise of a train allows Stanley to overhear Blanche and the chime of the cathedral contrasts with Blanche's desperate situation at the end of the play.
The volume of the sounds is turned up or down in correspondence with the dramatic events and emotional situation of the characters, for instance when Blanche is more or less haunted by the Varsouviana polka and the following shot. When Mitch is going to tell her that he cannot marry her, "the rapid, feverish polka tune, the 'Varsouviana', is heard" and reflects her "sense of disaster" (p. 86, l. 6). As only Blanche can hear that "the polka tune starts up again" and "the polka music dies out again" after the shot, Mitch believes that she is insane (cf. p. 87, ll. 20 ff). Before Stanley rapes Blanche, her fright is underlined by the "blue piano" that "begins to drum louder" and "turns into the roar of an approaching locomotive" (p. 98, ll. 25 f). The dramatist also uses music to link certain scenes such as Scene Five and Six, Scene Eight and Nine to underline that there is no break or fundamentally changing mood.
As Tennessee Williams intends to heighten the impact of the action his stage directions (cf. above Chapter III,3) convey a rather detailed picture of the

characters' appearance and behaviour, the atmosphere and the stage, its lighting and the sound effects. Most of these devices and effects can also be understood in a symbolic way (cf. Chapter III,4.9).
As violence is a major topic of the play, Tennessee Williams presents several violent scenes on stage such as the struggle of the poker players, Blanche's attempt at defending herself against Stanley with the top of a broken bottle and her scratching at the nurse who finally pinions her arms. But the more brutal scenes happen off-stage such as Stanley's hitting his pregnant wife and Blanche's rape. Since the row of Eunice and Steve is obviously meant to be comic, it can only be heard but its results including Steve's bruise, Eunice's fury and their peaceful return are shown on stage.
The playwright makes use of several comic elements in the play such as laughter and jokes. But frequently the laughter is hysterical or not meant seriously and the jokes are disgusting. When Blanche tells a funny story at her sullen birthday supper, she is the only one who laughs about it and thus stresses her isolation and despair.
The contrasting scenes stress the difference between Stanley's rude behaviour and Blanche's insistence on good manners. Whereas Stanley enjoys playing poker with his friends, Blanche calls it a "party of apes" and stresses the progress of mankind by mentioning "such things as art – as poetry and music – such kinds of new light" (p. 54, ll. 6 ff). When Stanley has no luck but loses at cards, Blanche is lucky to meet Mitch (cf. Scene Three) but at the end of the play when Stanley wins at cards, Blanche has lost Mitch. When Blanche is happily singing in the bathroom while Stanley informs his wife about her sister's past, contrast is used as a dramatic element to foreshadow Blanche's nervous breakdown and tragic fate. In his stage directions Tennessee Williams explains this dramatic device: "Blanche is singing in the bathroom a saccharine popular ballad which is used contrapunctally with Stanley's speech." (p. 74, ll. 4 f) The dramatist also underlines that after Stella spent the night with her husband though he had beaten her, Blanche "has spent a sleepless night and her appearance entirely contrasts with Stella's." (p. 47, ll. 12 f) The same dramatic device is for instance used when Blanche believes to meet Shep Huntleigh and talks about her outfit while Stella and Eunice arrange her being taken to a mental institution.
In order to prepare the audience or the readers for the following events and thus arouse or maintain the viewers' or readers' interest, the playwright foreshadows future events. At the beginning of the play he already alludes to Blanche's exterior and interior situation when Eunice asks her: "What's the matter, honey? Are you lost?" (p. 12, l. 26) As Blanche is, in fact, in a destitute situation and her last hope seems to be her sister's help, Eunice's question can be understood in a double sense and not only referring to Blanche's difficulties in finding Stella's apartment. When Mitch laments that his poker friends are married whereas he will be alone when his mother dies, Tennes-

see Williams foreshadows Mitch's wish to marry Blanche but also his being alone again after she is taken to the mental institution at the end of the play. Blanche also seems to see her being raped by Stanley and her mental breakdown coming when she thinks: "Of course there is such a thing as the hostility of – perhaps in some perverse kind of way he – No! To think of it makes me ..." (p. 69, ll. 33 ff). Stanley also alludes to his hidden sexual desire before raping her when he says: "We've had this date with each other from the beginning!" (p. 99, ll. 24 f) This might also refer to Blanche's attempt at flirting with him (cf. Scene Two). Tennessee Williams also alludes to Blanche's insanity at the end of the play by his choice of words before, e.g. nervous, lunacy, hysterical, crazy, insane, excitable, and Mitch's question "Are you boxed out of your mind?" Blanche and the audience are also aware of her mental instability, her nervousness and fright from the very beginning of the play. The motif of insanity is also used when Blanche calls Stanley a "madman" (p. 49, l. 3).
When Blanche talks about her past, the vivid and shocking description of her taking care of her dying relatives and the dramatic description of her husband's suicide remind of the cinematic device of a flashback.
In order to visualize Blanche's fright, confusion, panic and insanity at the end of the play Tennessee Williams makes use of various dramatic and cinematic effects. The struggle of a drunkard and a prostitute, which can be seen through the transparent back wall in the tenth scene and which seems to foreshadow the struggle of Stanley and Blanche, reminds of the cinematic device of cross-cutting or parallel action. Blanche's increasing fright of Stanley and her feeling of being in a trap are stressed by ghostly light effects and inhuman sounds: "Lurid reflections appear on the walls around Blanche. The shadows are of a grotesque and menacing form. [...] The night is filled with inhuman voices like cries in a jungle. The shadows and lurid reflections move sinuously as flames along the wall spaces." (p. 97, ll. 21 ff) Nearly the same light and sound effects accompany and mirror Blanche's panic and insanity in the last scene of the play: "Lurid reflections appear on the walls in odd, sinuous shapes. The 'Varsouviana' is filtered into a weird distortion, accompanied by the cries and noises of the jungle." (p. 105, ll. 27 ff) Moreover, the sinister Matron's "greeting is echoed and re-echoed by other mysterious voices behind the walls" (p. 106, ll. 1 f; cf. also ll. 13 f) and thus reflects Blanche's fright and insanity.

To sum up, the play is a skilful fabric of flashbacks, premonitions, cross-references, repetitions and allusions, which contribute to the strong emotional impact on the audience. In order to increase the dramatic effect of his play Tennessee Williams also links various dramatic and stylistic devices and for emphasis frequently attributes to them a different meaning or function.

7. Imagery and Symbolism

As Tennessee Williams also wrote numerous poems, he makes use of poetic devices in his plays. In *A Streetcar Named Desire* he frequently describes the atmosphere or the characters in his stage directions in a poetic way. Thus he employs images, metaphors, comparisons and symbols. The images, metaphors and comparisons are frequently also meant symbolically.

Symbols

In an essay which appeared in 1950 Tennessee Williams states that "art is made of symbols the way your body is made out of vital tissue" and that he frequently uses "symbols of the grotesque and the violent" because "the awfulness has to be compressed." (cf. *Essays*, p. 45) In his foreword to the play *Camino Royal* (1953) the playwright states: "I can't deny that I use a lot of those things called symbols but being a self-defensive creature, I say symbols are nothing but the natural speech of drama." (*Essays*, p. 66)
The "Blue Piano" which is "played with the infatuated fluency of brown fingers" (p. 10, ll. 13 f) and "expresses the spirit of the life" in the Vieux Carré symbolically accompanies the action throughout the play in different ways.
Already the title of the play suggests that the streetcar named Desire is symbolically used by the playwright and one of the major topics of the play is sexual desire, which affects all the characters. When for instance Blanche cannot understand why her sister spent the night with Stanley after being beaten by him, she says: "What you are talking about is brutal desire – just – Desire! – the name of that rattle-trap street-car that bangs through the Quarter, up one old narrow street and down another ..." (p. 52, ll. 33 ff)
Blanche, who tries to make Mitch desire her, repeats the name of the tram again when she returns disappointed from the night out with Mitch and – "laughing grimly" – ambiguously asks Mitch: "Is that street-car named Desire still grinding along the tracks at this hour?" (p. 64, ll. 17 f)
But since Blanche also uses the streetcar Cemeteries to arrive at Elysian Fields the dramatist – already at the beginning of the play – symbolically alludes to her own desire which will lead her to destruction after her sister's home has turned out to be a trap and no place of peace and protection. Elysian Fields is thus applied ironically since it seems to symbolize just the opposite.
The brand name of the whisky "Southern Comfort" (p. 88, l. 5) seems to symbolize Blanche's permanent attempt at calming her nerves and trying to drown her fears and sorrows in alcohol. Blanche takes hot baths throughout the play in order to calm her nerves. But the frequent use of water could also symbolize her wish to be purified from her sins, in particular from her feeling of guilt, which haunts her after her husband's suicide and which Tennessee Williams stresses by the polka music and the shot only Blanche can hear.

Tennessee Williams visualizes the characters by their clothes and the way they dress, which symbolizes their traits of character and their behaviour. Thus Blanche is characterized as delicate and fragile when the dramatist describes her graphically and poetically as "daintily dressed in a white suit with a fluffy bodice, necklace and earrings of pearl, white gloves and hat [...]. Her delicate beauty must avoid a strong light. There is something about her uncertain manner, as well as her white clothes, that suggests a moth." (p. 12, ll. 19 ff). Her white clothes also suggest innocence. But Blanche's other dresses, her costume jewellery and the episodes of dressing or undressing symbolize her vanity and wish to appear beautiful and deceive others. Moreover, her former promiscuous life in Laurel is mirrored. She needs fanciful clothes to hide her fading beauty and deceive Mitch into marrying her. Tennessee Williams symbolically employs the colours of butterfly wings to describe Blanche's wish to fascinate and deceive Mitch: "[Soft people] have got to be seductive – put on soft colors, the colors of butterfly wings, and glow – make a little – temporary magic just in order to pay for – one night's shelter!" (p. 58, ll. 23 ff)
Colours are frequently used symbolically such as the showy colours of the men's shirts, Blanche's white dress at the beginning of the play and the "soft colours of butterfly wings" she puts on to "glow" or to appear beautiful. When she wears "a red satin robe" (p. 28, l. 35), she wants to appear attractive and desired and begins to flirt with Stanley. When Eunice places the baby, who is wrapped in a blue blanket, in Stella's arms, Tennessee Williams makes use of the conventional blue colour to indicate that Stanley has got the son he wanted. But when Blanche corrects Stella and Eunice and calls the colour of her jacket "Della Robbia blue. The blue of the robe in the old Madonna pictures" (p. 103, ll. 6 f), the playwright seems to underline that Blanche desires to be pure and innocent.
Tennessee Williams does not only employ the streetcars symbolically but also the frightening noise of a locomotive, which the first time "thunders past" the house when Blanche tells Mitch about her discovery of Allan's homosexuality (cf. p. 71, ll. 11 ff) and loudly passes the house the second time when Stanley relentlessly rapes Blanche. The chime of the cathedral bells is considered "the only clean thing in the Quarter" by Blanche (p. 103, ll. 14 f).
Blanche can also be considered as a symbol of the refined but decadent Old South of plantation owners contrary to Stanley as the incarnation of the new and rather rude industrialized American South.
The metaphor of a moth also alludes to Blanche's fear of bright light and foreshadows the discovery of her true age by Mitch and her being threatened to be destroyed like a moth flying too near a light bulb. The naked bulb, however, symbolizes realism and the naked truth such as her true age, which Blanche tries to hide when she buys a Chinese paper lantern to cover the light bulb. But the paper lantern is not only a symbol of deceit but also symbolizes her wish to evade reality and replace it by imagination. She tells

Mitch: "I don't want realism. [...] I'll tell you what I want. Magic! [...] I don't tell the truth, I tell what *ought* to be truth." (p. 89, ll. 12 ff) Mitch's and Stanley's tearing the paper lantern off the bulb symbolizes their desire to be "realistic" but it also symbolizes Blanche's fright and tragic fate. In his stage directions Tennessee Williams finally points out that Blanche "cries out as if the lantern was herself" (p. 106, ll. 19 f). When she smashes her hand mirror the playwright symbolically underlines her fading beauty.
Tennessee Williams refers to death directly when Blanche describes her dying relatives and her husband's suicide. But already Blanche's transfer to the streetcar named Cemeteries in order to get to her sister's apartment at the street called Elysian Fields symbolically foreshadow Blanche's tragic end when she seems to be buried alive in a mental institution. Blanche believes that "the opposite of desire" is death and mentions the Grim Reaper, an allegory of death, when she tells about her traumatic experiences at Belle Reve. She is frightened by "a blind Mexican woman in a dark shawl" selling tin flowers and wreaths for funerals who seems to be a personification of death. Some critics also believe that grapes are a symbol of sexual desire and as Blanche fears to die from eating an unwashed grape this seems to be a parallel to the two streetcars of desire and death. Probably the name of the plantation is also meant in a symbolic way since its original name in correct French could have been Belle Rive (beautiful shore), "and that over the generations the name has been corrupted as the family's fortune dwindled. What had been a solid *shore* is now but an evanescent *dream* [French: rêve]of lost splendor." (Felicia Hardison Londré, p. 52)
Blanche's fright, panic and insanity are stressed by symbolic light effects and sounds. Whereas the lurid light and the ghostly shadows on the wall symbolize her panic and insanity, the sounds of the jungle and the noise of the locomotive stress Stanley's brutality and the rape. When the Matron greets Blanche, "the greeting is echoed and re-echoed by other mysterious voices" that seem to symbolize her panic and insanity. But at the end of the play she regains her composure and "walks on without turning", which symbolizes that she has not lost her human dignity.

Images, metaphors and comparisons

In his stage directions Tennessee Williams describes the French Quarter in a poetic and graphic way. He stresses its "raffish charm" and the sky's "peculiarly tender blue, almost a turquoise, which invests the scene with a kind of lyricism and gracefully attenuates the atmosphere of decay." When Blanche vividly describes her desperate situation at Belle Reve in Scene One, Tennessee Williams again employs detailed images of decay.
Blanche describes Stanley's primitive character and behaviour in Scene Four as "sub-human". Already in Scene One when Stanley throws raw meat up to

Stella, the return of a Stone Age hunter is alluded to. Blanche calls Stanley a "survivor of the stone age! Bearing the raw meat home from the kill in the jungle!" (p. 53, ll. 34 f). She even uses the metaphor "devil" for desire when she expresses her disgust of Stella's relationship to her husband and also seems to allude to herself (cf. p. 53, l. 6). Stella calls him a "powder-keg" (p. 48, l. 19) since he is easily enraged when he drinks too much. Stanley, however, who does not treat his wife as an equal partner, calls her "baby doll" while the music is symbolically playing "Paper Doll" (cf. p. 44, ll. 26, 23).

Tennessee Williams also describes the atmosphere of the poker night in a graphic and rather poetic way when the kitchen "suggests that sort of lurid nocturnal brilliance, the raw colors of childhood's spectrum" and the players as men "at the peak of their physical manhood, as coarse and direct and powerful as the primary colors." (p. 35, ll. 8 f) Whereas Blanche is metaphorically called a "moth" at the beginning of the play, Stanley is metaphorically characterized as "a richly feathered male bird among hens" and as a "gaudy seed-bearer." At the end of Scene Four Blanche metaphorically describes the poker players and in particular Stanley as "apes" since she believes that they are primitive and uncultivated. Their animal-like behaviour is vividly presented by an image of Stone Age life.

Images or metaphorical style are frequently used to convey a graphic picture of the characters' feelings, e.g. when Stella says: "My head is swimming" (p. 27, l. 7) or Mitch criticizes Stanley as sitting "on your high horse" (p. 35, l. 29). Stanley uses various images and metaphorical sayings when he informs Stella about Blanche's past, e.g. "the cat's out of the bag" (p. 73, l. 32),"to pull the wool over one's eyes" (p. 75, l. 6; cf. also p. 97, ll. 13 f), "to call somebody on the carpet" and "They had her on the hook" (p. 76, ll. 14 ff). As he wants to warn Mitch Stanley uses the metaphorical phrase "to jump in a tank with a school of sharks" (p. 78, l. 14) and finally hypocritically offers Blanche to make peace: "Shall we bury the hatchet and make a loving-cup?" (p. 95, l. 18) Blanche also uses metaphorical phrases that stress her imagination such as "[They] have tied an old tin can to the tail of a kite" (p. 90, l. 26) or "Dallas where gold spouts out of the ground" (p. 94, ll. 36 f). She also employs metaphorical style that implies religious aspects such as "The poor man's Paradise – is a little peace" (p. 90, l. 24) or "to cast one's pearls before swine" (p.96, ll. 13 f), which is based on the Bible, Matthew 7:6.

As Tennessee Williams wants to convey a graphic impression to the audience or readers, he frequently uses comparisons and similes. Blanche for instance humorously compares her sister to a partridge since she has put on weight and compares her to a baby without knowing that Stella is pregnant (cf. p. 17, l. 10). When Stella appears to be quiet and peaceful, Blanche compares her to "a cherub in choir" (p. 17, ll. 25 f). When she tells Stanley the lie that she is invited to a Caribbean cruise, Tennessee Williams employs the simile "It came like a bolt from the blue" (p. 94, l. 15). When the soldiers who make love to Blanche are taken to the camp by a paddy-wagon, Tennessee Williams ironically compares it to gathering them up like daisies (p. 91, ll. 28 f). Mitch tells Blanche that Stanley believes that she has been "lapping" his whisky up "like a wild-cat" (p. 88, ll. 18 f), which also has a comic effect. When Mitch waltzes awkwardly he is compared to a "dancing bear" (p. 43, l. 5) and Stanley to a "baying hound" (p. 45, l. 1) when he shouts for Stella.

8. Language and Stylistic Devices

Tennessee Williams employs different varieties of American English, foreign languages such as French and Spanish and various stylistic devices. Images and symbols are also stylistic devices but are dealt with in the previous chapter because of their specific relevance for Tennessee Williams.

Language varieties and extra-verbal sounds

The dramatist employs American English, which can be easily recognized because of the American spelling of several words that differs from British English such as -or for -our (color, favor, glamor, neighbors), -er for -re (center), one consonant for two (traveling, jewelry), -s- for -c- (offense), -y for -ey (story instead of storey). Some words differ from British English, e. g. streetcar (tram), tracks (rails), porch (veranda), sidewalk (pavement), intermingle (mix), purse (handbag), bar (pub), graveyard (cemetery), stove (cooker), bureau (chest of drawers), allowance (pocket money), rooster (cock), drug-store, overwrought, outburst, etc.

The playwright also mentions some American cities such as New Orleans, Laurel and Dallas, the French Quarter, street names such as Elysian Fields and Bourbon (street) in New Orleans and Biscayne Boulevard (in Miami), the former Louisville and Nashville railroad and the Greyhound long-distance coach company, the Gulf (of Mexico) and the Caribbean sea, etc. Thus Tennessee Williams conveys an authentic geographical background to the play and the characters' life or dreams. He also employs the broad Southern accent sometimes, for instance when the negation "No" is replaced by "Naw". And Steve imitates the black people's accent when he tells a joke about an "ole nigger" who says: "Lord God, I hopes I never gits *that* hongry." (p. 36, ll. 20 ff) Though "nigger" is a very offensive word, Steve seems to use it thoughtlessly as a slang expression.

Corresponding to the multicultural city of New Orleans the dramatist also uses French words such as Mardi Gras, Creole French such as Belle Reve (correct French: Beau Rêve) and mentions Mexican and Chinese food, tamale and chop suey. The German opera title "Rosenkavalier" is used by Blanche to describe Mitch when he appears with red roses (though in the opera it is a silver rose) and the German loanword "kibitz" is used by her when she wishes to look at the poker cards.

Spanish is used for instance to underline the Mexican origin of many people living in the multicultural city of New Orleans such as Pablo, the tamale vendor and the Mexican woman who sells funeral flowers.

Contrary to the other characters Blanche speaks French and even exclaims the Greek *Eureka!* because she wants to appear an educated woman. Tennessee Williams also stresses her imagination and dreams when she imagines living a Bohemian life and enjoying *joie de vivre* in Paris and compares herself in French with *la Dame aux Camellias* (correct: *Camélias*) and Mitch with her lover Armand. But at the same time this comparison alludes to the French lady's promiscuity and tragic fate and death. Thus the playwright might allude to the multiple facets of Blanche's character as he frequently does and also seems to foreshadow Blanche's tragic end. Moreover, she asks improper questions in French such as "Voulez-vous couchez [correct: coucher] avec moi ce soir?" because Mitch cannot understand her but at the same time she – in a coquettish way – seems to express that she desires him (cf. p. 66, ll. 18 ff).

Moreover, the dramatist uses different varieties of American English. Whereas Blanche and Stella usually speak Standard American English, Stanley, his friends and other characters generally use colloquialisms and non-standard language such as slang, e.g. clip-joint (disreputable bar), honky-tonk, hoity-toity, dandy (super, great), to have a gander at sth (to have a look at sth), You're damn tootin' (absolutely), toots (darling), cut the re-bop (stop the nonsense), sugar-tit (sexy woman), head (toilet), bobby soxer (teenager), hooey (stupid talk), loco (mad), malarky (exaggerated talk, lies), rough house (fight), etc.

In comparison with Standard American English, their speech is frequently grammatically wrong, for instance when they say: "We was together", "set" instead of "sit", "them" instead of "these". Moreover, they use forms such as gonna (going to), gotta (got to), ain't (aren't or haven't), double negatives, for instance "She didn't show you no papers", abbreviations such as "cig" for cigarette. They also omit sounds, e.g. th'ew (threw), which is meant to be Creole English, and leave out words, e.g. "I'll go tell her you come".

Thus the dramatist underlines that Stanley and his friends belong to the working class contrary to Blanche's and Stella's "aristocratic" social background. But whereas Stella is trying to adapt to her new social situation, Blanche tries to keep up the facade of conventional manners and education. Like Tennessee Williams in his stage directions she likes to employ an elaborate language and uses words such as "expose" instead of show, "proceed" for continue and "toilette" for clothes and make-up. Moreover, she stresses her level of education by the use of French words and sentences or even refers to Latin by explaining the Latin meaning of her sister's name or the name of the hotel Tarantula or using special terms such as "hydro-therapy". But when she insults Stanley she also employs an unrefined language like him.

Stanley and his friends except Mitch use various rude expressions such as "ass" or swear words such as "damned". Even Blanche, whose speech is often refined, uses offensive words to degrade Stanley, e.g. Polack, pig, ape, bestial, common and vulgar. Also Eunice and Stella make use of offensive expressions when they are angry. On the other hand Stella and Blanche employ some euphemisms to be gentle or make something seem more acceptable, e.g. "four-letter-word" for fuck, "I'll take to the streets" instead of prostitution, "familiarity" instead of sexual touch, "to pass on" for to die, "degenerate" for homosexual, "intimacies" for sex. When Blanche meets Mitch in front of the bathroom and calls it "The Little Boys' Room", her use of this euphemism seems to indicate that Blanche wants to stress her good manners, though it also has a comic effect. Possibly Tennessee Williams also prevented the use of offensive and taboo words and expressions that could be considered obscene or shocking by the audience though Steve uses the taboo word "nigger" three times when he tells a dirty joke.
In order to convey an authentic impression of spoken language Tennessee Williams employs colloquialisms or informal speech such as "Are you kidding?" or the addresses "honey" and "baby", short sentences, abbreviations such as "Pre-Med", elliptical remarks such as "She here?" and one-word commands, questions and replies, for instance: "Catch! – What? – Meat!" But "Stell" for Stella is also used by Blanche and Stanley to stress their affection. Frequently the characters interrupt each other and continue or complete the other character's remark or question. Extra-verbal expressions are used to express emotions or thoughts such as "Hah!" to express contempt, "Hey!" to attract attention or "Huh?" instead of "What?" "Ha-ha" frequently indicates laughter, "Oh" expresses surprise or fear and "Hush" is used instead of "Silence". Blanche utters "Ouuuuu" because she cannot bear Stanley's loud voice or "Hmmmmm" when she investigates the papers about the plantation.

Stylistic devices

Figurative words and phrases are used to convey a more vivid impression of the situation or the emotions of the characters, e.g. "lay one's cards on the table" instead of "to tell the truth" or "he was in the quicksands" for "he needed help", "My youth was suddenly gone up the water-spout", "fishing for compliments" (p. 26), etc.
When Stanley and his friends play poker, they use special terms and short remarks such as "Anything wild this deal? – One-eyed jacks are wild. – Give me two cards. – You Mitch? – I'm out. – One. [...]" Stanley uses the legal term Napoleonic Code several times to stress his right to be informed about the loss of Belle Reve. Special military terms are employed to describe Stanley's commitment in World War II as an officer.

Moreover, the words employed by Tennessee Williams are taken from various fields to describe the atmosphere in New Orleans or to express the characters' emotions and knowledge. The dramatist for instance mentions the music and the musical instruments that a characteristic of New Orleans and also reflect his characters' emotions. Blanche for instance refers to writers, literature, art and music. Numerous words describing factory work, clothes, entertainment, or referring to religion (e.g. God, Bible, Samson, St Barnabas) are used. The names of animals are metaphorically employed, e.g. by Blanche who uses "pig" and "ape" to insult Stanley, "lamb" to kindly address Stella and "wolf" to get to know whether Mitch is married. At the same time the animals' names allude to certain traits of character since Blanche and even Stella criticize Stanley's bad manners or his primitive behaviour, Blanche describes her sister as patient and soft and Mitch is just the opposite of a "wolf" until his attempt at raping Blanche. As Stanley only cares for himself and does not care for others Mitch calls him a "bull."

Tennessee Williams frequently makes use of comic effects, humour and irony, either in connection with other stylistic devices or directly, for instance when Steve tells dirty jokes or he quarrels with his wife. When Stanley describes Blanche's fox fur as "half a mile long" or Blanche tells that Shep Huntleigh's Cadillac "must have been a block long", the dramatist's use of hyperbole has a comic effect. Stanley ridicules someone who could open bottles with his teeth until he lost them as a "human bottle opener." Also Blanche has a sense of humour and irony when she for instance ridicules the wives of Stanley's friends because of their weight or laughs about her illusionary letter to Shep Huntleigh and the proverb "Forewarned is forearmed" or says: "I understand there's to be a little card party to which we ladies are cordially *not* invited" or quotes from the Bible: "The blind are – leading the blind!" But her irony is rather bitter when she addresses her sister as "Miss Stella" because she left her alone at Belle Reve or when she tells Mitch that she behaved like a spider and brought her "victims" to the hotel Tarantula. It is gallows humour when she – as she believes – tells a funny story after being stood up by Mitch and is the only one who laughs about it.

Though Blanche calls Stanley common and primitive, Stanley frequently employs irony, for instance when he uses the word play "Some people rarely touch it [alcohol], but it touches them often." When Stanley is upset because of Blanche's expensive clothes and jewellery as he believes, he ironically asks his wife if her sister is "a deep-sea diver who brings up sunken treasures" or "the champion safe-cracker of all time." He ironically calls Blanche "her Majesty" because she is served by Stella or "Dame Blanche" because of her claim to be a lady despite her disreputable past in Laurel, where she was as famous "as if she was the President of the United States." He ironically calls her "visiting royalty" and asks her if she believes to be "Queen of the Nile" (i. e. Cleopatra) "sitting on a throne."

Repetition is frequently used to stress ideas and emotions, e. g. when Blanche repeats "I, I, *I*", "I know, I know", "The loss – the loss", "Saw! Saw!" Stella is shocked at her husband's birthday present for Blanche and repeats: "What will she do!" because she feels pity for her sister and would like to help her. She also repeats "It will" five times to encourage Blanche when she hopes to marry Mitch. But when Blanche wants to know what Stanley told his wife about Laurel, Stella repeats: "Nothing, nothing, nothing!" though it is a lie. Thus the dramatist employs repetition either to underline something true, for instance a true idea or emotion felt by a character, e. g. when Blanche repeats the negation "No" at the beginning of the play. But she also repeats something, e. g. that she only drinks a little whisky, to make Stanley believe it though he recognizes the opposite. The dramatist stresses Stanley's selfishness when Stanley starts bragging that he is lucky and repeats the first person singular five times.

But Tennessee Williams does not merely repeat words or phrases for emphasis but employs them in different ways such as the word "baby". Stella compares herself to a crying baby when Stanley is not with her. Stanley addresses Stella as his baby or "baby doll" as if she were a plaything. The dramatist alludes to Stella's pregnancy when Blanche compares her to a "partridge". Blanche is shocked when Stanley beats his pregnant wife and Eunice accuses him: "You can't beat on a woman [...]. And her goin' t' have a baby!" When Mitch attacks Stanley, Stanley shouts: "Hold this bone-headed cry-baby!" At the end of the play the playwright replaces the word baby by "child", when Eunice places the little boy in Stella's arms, which symbolically emphasizes her idea that life must go on and "Stella accepts the child, sobbingly" (p. 108, ll. 10 f).

Enumeration is for instance used when Stanley informs his wife about Blanche's life in Laurel: "Lie Number One [...] Lie Number Two [...]" to structure the information and stress the reliability of his sources. He also enumerates different people or experts who can inform him about Blanche's life in Laurel and about the value of her jewellery. But when Blanche enumerates the dead and lists numerous exclamations, Tennessee Williams stresses her strong emotions and accusations.

Exclamations stress the characters' strong emotions or their dramatic behaviour. Stanley for instance commands "Shut up!" and "Sit down!" or "Get out of the bathroom!" and yearningly exclaims his wife's name five times when she fled to Eunice. The increasing volume of his voice and his despair is signalled by the unusual writing of his wife's name in capital letters (cf. p. 45, l. 16). When Eunice is upset about her husband, she exclaims: "I'm gonna call the police!" and repeats it but does not do it. Blanche for instance exclaims: "Get out of here quick before I start screaming Fire!" and repeats it when Mitch does not leave until she "cries wildly Fire! Fire! Fire!" though she does not really call the fire brigade but reacts hysterically.

Exclamations that contain religious names are frequently employed throughout the play and underscore the characters' emotions. They are used as swear words or to express despair, fear, helplessness, loneliness, happiness, etc. Stanley for instance curses "Goddamn" when he is upset about Blanche's hot baths or "Aw, for the sake of Jesus, go home, then!" when he is angry about Mitch, who exclaims "Christ!" when he is deeply disappointed in Blanche. "Oh God!" is frequently used to express despair. Religious words are used in different contexts to stress something as positive such as man as God's image, Stella's baby as sleeping like an angel, Stella's tranquillity compared with Eastern idols or Blanche's belief that her soul will be transported to heaven.

Tennessee Williams frequently employs antithesis and contrast to describe the differences between the characters, to stress the conflicts between them or the problems they have to cope with, for instance between realism and magic, truth and illusion, life and death, youth and age, bad manners and etiquette, violence and softness, desire and love, primitiveness and human progress, honesty and deceit. The contrast between Blanche and Stanley and Stella is for instance underlined by their standard of education and their pass time activities. Whereas Stanley seems to be only interested in bowling and poker and Stella looks at coloured comics, which stresses her adaptation to Stanley's level of education, Blanche mentions or alludes to famous poets and writers such as Hawthorne, Whitman and Poe (cf. p. 42, l. 28). But when she mentions them she also underlines that most of her former students are not interested in literature but in "love". Blanche stresses that she does not want to be realistic like Stanley or Mitch because their "reality" is primitive and violent. She desires a different kind of reality, which exists in her mind as a better world but is in fact illusionary. She romantically mentions the Pleiades and seems to believe in astrology when she refers to Aries to describe Stanley's noisy behaviour or mentions her astrological sign, Virgo, possibly to pretend that she is a virgin, which Stanley ridicules. She also seems to believe in numerology or the occult significance of numbers.

When Blanche quotes the refrain from Poe's poem "Ulalume" (cf. p. 16, ll. 1 ff) to describe the Kowalskis' home though the poet's line refers to horror and death Blanche is laughing about her "joke". Thus Tennessee Williams language use is ambiguous. Blanche also knows that the inscription on Mitch's silver case is taken from a sonnet by Elizabeth Barrett Browning (p. 40, l. 27) and again the playwright seems to use Browning's line ambiguously since it refers to love and death. It applies to Mitch's loss of his girl and seems to foreshadow his loss of Blanche at the end of the play. Moreover, Blanche mentions the Tales of 1001 Nights, which stresses her romantic trait of character, and the opera *Rosenkavalier* by Richard Strauss (cf. p. 63, l. 5). But when she compares Mitch with a "Rosenkavalier" because he appears with red roses in his hands, Tennessee Williams underlines her wishful thinking

and her sticking to conventional behaviour. Though Blanche stresses her level of education as a teacher, she also sings popular songs when she is taking a hot bath.
Alliteration is used to stress an idea, for instance “I stayed and struggled” (p. 20, l. 7), “feathers and furs” (p. 27, l. 28), “prim and proper” (p. 60, l. 20). To increase the effect of her words Blanche uses an intensifying and rather melodramatic style: “I stayed and fought for it, bled for it, almost died for it!” which Stella calls a “hysterical outburst” (cf. p. 20, ll. 15 ff).
As Blanche also uses slang sometimes and insulting words though she demands politeness and gallantry and Stanley and Stella also tell lies and deceive Blanche, Tennessee Williams underlines that the characters do not really stand in an extreme contrast to each other but frequently behave inconsistently. Blanche for instance contradicts herself when she states that she is “not meaning this in a reproachful way” and then continues to reproach her sister. Thus the dramatist presents mixed characters and not types who make it easy to recognize what they really mean.

To sum up, Tennessee Williams employs various stylistic devices to stress his characters’ thoughts, emotions and behaviour or to convey a graphic impression of them. But in many cases he does not use these devices in a specific sense only but ambiguously or ironically or he makes use of various effects at the same time. The readers and the audience are supposed to be aware of the undercurrent meanings of the characters’ words, their multiple traits and inconsistent or contradictory behaviour. Tennessee Williams himself pointed out that “some mystery should be left in the revelation of character in a play, just as a great deal of mystery is always left in the revelation of character in life, even in one’s own character to himself.” (*Essays*, p. 72)

IV Tennessee Williams and Elia Kazan on *A Streetcar Named Desire*

Though Tennessee Williams frequently points out that he does not comment on his play, he gives his opinion about it and its characters several times. As he cooperated with Elia Kazan, the stage director of the play in New York and the director of its cinematic adaptation, both the playwright's and the stage and film director's views are documented.

1. Tennessee Williams' Remarks about the Play

1.1 Memoirs

In his *Memoirs* the dramatist describes how he started to write the play but was not able to continue writing it:

> "Almost directly after *Menagerie* went into rehearsals I started upon a play whose first title was *Blanche's Chair in the Moon*. But I did only a single scene for it that winter of 1944–45 in Chicago. In that scene Blanche was in some steaming hot Southern town, sitting alone in a chair with the moonlight coming through a window on her, waiting for a beau who didn't show up. I stopped working on it because I became mysteriously depressed and debilitated and you know how hard it is to work in that condition. I decided not to drink black coffee and not to work for several months and I really did stick to that self-promise." (p. 86)

But in the autumn of 1946 when Tennessee Williams stayed in New Orleans he continued writing the play: "I took up where I'd left off with *Streetcar*, which I was then calling *The Poker Night*. I wrote furiously on it. For despite the fact that I thought I was dying, or maybe because of it, I had a great passion for work. I would work from early morning until early afternoon, and then, spent from the rigors of creation, I would go around the corner to a bar called Victor's and revive myself with a marvelous drink [...]" (pp. 109 f), which reminds of Blanche's behaviour to a certain extent. But when he read the first draft to his grandfather and some friends, "they were shocked by it. And so was I." He went to Key West and "really began to get *Streetcar* into shape. It went like a house on fire" (p. 111). He finished the play and mailed

it to his representative Audrey Wood whose answer was "much more positive and encouraging" this time (cf. p. 111). The play was produced by Irene Selznick and directed by Elia Kazan. After they had decided that Marlon Brando should play the part of Stanley and Jessica Tandy the part of Blanche, the two most important roles, Tennessee Williams "told Kazan that he should cast the rest of the parts as he wished" (cf. pp. 130 ff).
When Tennessee Williams went to New York where the rehearsals of the play progressed, he "thought that the play was a certain failure" and he "was again certain that he was a dying artist and not even the least bit sure that I [he] was an artist" (p. 134). He seemed to be right because its opening in New Haven in November 1947 was hardly noticed and Thornton Wilder, the famous writer of *Our Town*, told him that the play was based "on a fatally mistaken premise. No female who has ever been a lady (he was referring to Stella) could possibly marry a vulgarian such as Stanley" (p. 136). The next performance in Boston got good notices and the performance in Philadelphia was a success. When Elia Kazan said: "This smells like a hit" (p. 137), he was right because in New York the play was a "smash" and ran for 855 performances.
In his *Memoirs* Tennessee Williams identifies with Blanche several times because she personifies some of his own traits of character. He admits that he is "as much of an hysteric as [...] Blanche" (p. 117), that there has always been in him "the conviction of Blanche, that deliberate cruelty is the one unforgivable thing" (p. 170) and that Blanche's last words "I have always depended upon the kindness of strangers" also apply to himself: "Actually it was true, I always had, and without being often disappointed. In fact, I would guess that chance acquaintances, or strangers, have usually been kinder to me than friends – which does not speak too well for me." (p. 131)

He quotes and explains Blanche's answer to Mitch who believes that she is not "straight" (cf. *Streetcar*, p. 89, ll. 26 ff): "What is straight? A line can be straight, or a street, but the human heart, oh, no, it's curved like a road through mountains!" (pp. 53 f) Thus the playwright underlines that he presents complex characters and not "types". He points out that Blanche's feelings were "too great for her to contain without the escape of madness" (p. 235).

1.2 Letters

In a letter to his agent Audrey Wood Tennessee Williams wrote in New Orleans when he stayed there in the French Quarter in 1946, he mentions four working titles of the play and gives a short summary of its background (cf. Leverich, pp. 580 f):

> "I have been buried in work the last week or so and am about 55 or 60 pages into the first draft of a play which I am trying to design for Cornell [the actress

Katherine Cornell]. At the moment it has four different titles, The Moth, The Poker Night, The Primary Colors, or Blanche's Chair in The Moon. It is about two sisters, the remains of a fallen southern family. The younger, Stella, has accepted the situation, married beneath her socially and moved to a southern city with her coarsely attractive, plebeian mate. But Blanche (the Cornell part) has remained at Belle-reve, the home place in ruins, and struggles for five years to maintain the old order. Though essentially decent and very delicate by nature, she has gone for protection to various men till her name is tarnished. She teaches English in a small-town high-school but loses her job when her name is involved with a married man's. The place is finally lost, Belle-reve, and Blanche, destitute, gives up the struggle and takes refuge with Stella in the southern city."

Before *A Streetcar Named Desire* was produced for the stage in New York, Tennessee Williams tries to clarify his "intentions in the play" in his letter of April 19, 1947 to the stage director, Elia Kazan, whose nickname was Gadge (cf. *Letters*, Vol. II, pp. 95 f):

Dear Gadge:

[...]
I am sure that you must also have had reservations about the script. I will try to clarify my intentions in this play. I think its best quality is its authenticity or its fidelity to life. There are no "good" or "bad" people. Some are a little better or a little worse but all are activated more by misunderstanding than malice. A blindness to what is going on in each other's hearts. Stanley sees Blanche not as a desperate, driven creature backed into a last corner to make a last desperate stand – but as a calculating bitch with "round heels". Mitch accepts first her own false projection of herself as a refined young virgin, saving herself for the one eventual mate – then jumps way over to Stanley's conception of her. Nobody sees anybody truly, but all through the flaws of their own ego. That is the way we all see each other in life. Vanity, fear, desire, competition – all such distortions within our own egos – condition our vision of those in relation to us. Add to those distortions in our own egos, the corresponding distortions in the egos of the others – and you see how cloudy the glass must become through which we look at each other. That's how it is in all living relationships except when there is that rare case of two people who love intensely enough to burn through all those layers of opacity and see each other's naked hearts. Such a case seems purely theoretical to me.

However in creative fiction and drama, if the aim is fidelity, people are shown as we never see them in life but as they are. Quite impartially, without any ego-flaws in the eye of the beholder. We see from outside what could not be seen within, and the truth of the tragic dilemma becomes apparent. It was not that one person was bad or good, one right or wrong, but that all judged falsely concerning each other, what seemed black to one and white to the other is actually grey – a perception that could occur only through the detached eye of art. (As if a ghost sat over the affairs of men and made a true record of them.) Naturally a play of this kind does not exactly present a theme or score a point, unless it be the point or theme of human misunderstanding. When you begin to arrange the action of a play to score a certain point the fidelity to life may suffer. I don't say it always does. Things may be selected to score a point clearly without any contrivance toward that end, but I am afraid it happens rarely.

Finding a director aside from yourself who can bring this play to life exactly as if it were happening in life is going to be a problem. But that is the kind of direction it has to have. (I don't necessarily mean "realism": sometimes a living quality is caught better by expressionism than what is supposed to be realistic treatment.)

I remember you asked me what should an audience feel for Blanche. Certainly pity. It is a tragedy with the classic aim of producing a katharsis of pity and terror, and in order to do that Blanche must finally have the understanding and compassion of the audience. This without creating a black-dyed villain in Stanley. It is a thing (misunderstanding) not a person (Stanley) that destroys her in the end. In the end you should feel – "If only they all had known about each other!" – But there was always the paper lantern or the naked bulb!

(Incidentally, at the close of the play, I think Stanley should remove the paper lantern from the bulb – after Blanche is carried out and as he goes to resume the game.)

I have written all this out in case you were primarily troubled over my intention in the play. Please don't regard this as "pressure". [...]

Sincerely,
Tennessee

After the stage production of *A Streetcar Named Desire* Tennessee Williams writes a letter to Justin Brooks Atkinson, the author of the *New York Times* article of December 14, 1947 (cf. Chapter VI, 5.1), in which he underlines that the playwright has exposed a desperate woman to "an alien environment that brutally wears on her nerves" but that he takes "no sides in the conflict". Moreover, he points out that the "uniformity" shown to date in the "choice of characters and in the attitude toward life ... may limit the range of Mr. Williams' career as a playwright." (cf. *Letters*, Vol. II, p. 138). At the end of the letter the playwright mentions that he is soon leaving for Europe. The reason why he left New York soon after the great success of *A Streetcar Named Desire* is given in his *Memoirs* (p. 139): "At the end of that December, no longer able to cope with the unremitting publicity in New York, I sailed for Europe." This corresponds to his view of success he published four days before the play's performance (cf. Tennessee Williams: *On A Streetcar Named Success*; cf. Chapter VI, 2).

Dear Brooks:

At last a criticism which connects directly with the essence of what I thought was the play! I mean your Sunday article which I have just read with deepest satisfaction of any the play's success has given me. So many of the others, saying 'alcoholic', 'nymphomaniac', 'prostitute', 'boozy' and so forth seemed – though stirred by the play – to be completely off the track, or nearly so. I wanted to show that people are not definable in such terms but are things of multiple facets and all but endless complexity that they do not fit "any convenient label" and are seldom more than partially visible even to those who live just on the other side of "the portieres".

You have also touched on my main problem: expanding my material and my interests. I can't answer that question. I know it and fear it and can only make more effort to extend my "feelers" beyond what I've felt so far. Thank you, Brooks. I am leaving for Europe soon. I will get in touch with you and Orianne before I sail.

Yours, Tenn.

In a letter of November 2, 1948 to Jessica Tandy, who played the part of Blanche during the first performances of the play in New York, Tennessee Williams underlines that it is Blanche in particular who he loved and wanted to present on the stage. He expresses his shame that he first supported Thomas Hart Benton's painting of the Poker Night scene with Blanche in a seductive posture, which emphasizes sex and brutality. He criticizes the superficiality of audiences that only recognize these aspects of a play. Though he tolerates the painting since it truly presents one side of the play, he underscores a more refined approach (cf. *Letters*, Vol. II, p. 213).

Dear Jessica:

Many, many thanks for your letter on the Benton picture. You are so right that it really makes me ashamed of having lent my casual support to the idea. What you say about Blanche suddenly recalls to me all of my original conception of the character and what it was to me, from which you, in your delineation, have never once drifted away in spite of what I now realize must have been a continual pressure: that unwillingness of audiences to share a more intricate and special and sensitive response to things: their desire to participate more safely, familiarly, in the responses of an animal nature. I have almost forgotten (perhaps under this same pressure) that it was Blanche whom I loved and respected and whom I wished to portray, though I have never, please believe me, forgotten the exact and tender and marvelously understanding way that you brought her to life. – I have such a divided nature! Irreconciliably divided. I look at Benton's picture and I see the strong things in it, its immediate appeal to the senses, raw, sensual, dynamic, and I forgot the play was really about those things which are opposed to that, the delicate half-approaches to something much finer. Yes, the painting is only one side of the play, and the Stanley side of it. Perhaps from the painter's point of view that was inevitable. A canvas cannot depict two worlds very easily: or the tragic division of the human spirit: at least not a painter of Benton's realistic type. Well, I am still an admirer of the painting, but, believe me, still more an admirer of yours for seeing and feeling about it more clearly than I did at first, and I should have felt the same way.

With love, Tennessee.

2. Elia Kazan, *Notebook for "A Streetcar Named Desire"*

In his *Memoirs* (p. 135) Tennessee Williams points out that Elia Kazan "was one of those rare directors who wanted the playwright around at all rehearsals, even those at which he was blocking out the action. Once in a while he would call me up on stage to demonstrate how I felt a certain bit should be played. I suspect he did this only to flatter me for he never had the least uncertainty in his work, once he had started upon it. I remember his asking me to demonstrate my conception of the old Mexican woman who passed along the street selling brilliant tin flowers for graves, calling out and chanting, '*Flores para los muertos, corones para los muertos.*' I got up on the rehearsal stage and advanced to the door of the Kowalski abode bearing the tin flowers ... Jessica opened the door and screamed at the sight of me. 'Not yet, not yet!' 'That's it, do it just like that,' said Kazan."
As Tennessee Williams and Elia Kazan closely cooperated to put *A Streetcar Named Desire* on stage, the stage director's ideas about the play, which he wrote down in his Notebook, also reflect the dramatist's conception of the tragedy to a large extent. Moreover, their cooperation contributed to the great success of the play, which ran for 855 performances in New York.
The following extracts from his *Notebook for "A Streetcar Named Desire"* dated August 1947, which he kept before and during the rehearsals, refer to Elia Kazan's search for the inner spirit of the play, which he believed was founded on understanding the "spine" of each character, i.e. the essential characteristic. That is why he analyzes and describes the four major characters of the play from his own point of view, which is certainly not totally identical with the playwright's conception but was obviously tolerated by Tennessee Williams as an effective way of putting his play on stage. As different people may –at least to a certain extent – understand a piece of literature in a different way, it could be useful to critically compare Elia Kazan's views with the playwright's rather few remarks on his play. Moreover, their views could also be compared with one's own interpretation and also with some reviews and some views of literary critics. (cf. Chapter V).

Extracts from Elia Kazan's *Notebook* (cf. Cole/Chinoy, *Directors on Directing*, pp. 365–379)

This play is a poetic tragedy. We are shown the final dissolution of a person of worth, who once had great potential, and who, even as she goes down, has worth exceeding that of the "healthy", coarse-grained figures who kill her.

Blanche is a social type, an emblem of a dying civilization, making its last curlicued and romantic exit. All her behavior patterns are those of the dying civilization she represents. In other words her behavior is *social*. Therefore find social modes! This is the source of the play's stylization and the production's style and color. Likewise Stanley's behavior is *social* too. It is the basic animal cynicism of today. "Get what's coming to you! Don't waste a day! Eat, drink, get yours!" This is the basis of his stylization, of the choice of his props. All props should be stylized: they should have a color, shape and weight that spell: style.

An effort to put poetic names on scenes to edge me into stylizations and physicalizations. Try to keep each scene in terms of Blanche.

1. Blanche comes to the last stop at the end of the line.
2. Blanche tries to make a place for herself.
3. Blanche breaks them apart, but when they come together, Blanche is more alone than ever!
4. Blanche, more desperate because more excluded, tries the direct attack and makes the enemy who will finish her.
5. Blanche finds that she is being tracked down for the kill. She must work fast.
6. Blanche suddenly finds, suddenly makes for herself, the only possible, perfect man for her.
7. Blanche comes out of the happy bathroom to find that her own doom has caught up with her.
8. Blanche fights her last fight. Breaks down. Even Stella deserts her.
9. Blanche's last desperate effort to save herself by telling the whole truth. The *truth dooms* her.
10. Blanche escapes out of this world. She is brought back by Stanley and destroyed.
11. Blanche is disposed of.

The style – the real deep style – consists of one thing only: to find behavior that's truly social, significantly typical, at each moment. It's not so much what

Blanche has done – it's how she does it – with such style, grace, manners, old-world trappings and effects, props, tricks, swirls, etc., that they seem anything but vulgar.

[...]

Blanche

"Blanche is Desperate"

"This is the End of the Line of the Streetcar Named Desire"

Spine – find Protection: the tradition of the old South says that it must be through another person.

Her problem has to do with her tradition. Her notion of what a woman should be. She is stuck with this "ideal." It is her ego. Unless she lives by it, she cannot live; in fact her whole life has been for nothing. Even the Alan Gray [correct: [Allan Grey] incident as she now tells it and believes it to have been, is a necessary piece of romanticism. Essentially, in outline, she tells what happened, but it also serves the demands of her notion of herself, to make her *special* and different, out of the tradition of the romantic ladies of the past [...]. This way it serves as an excuse for a great deal of her behavior.

Because this image of herself cannot be accomplished in reality, certainly not in the South of our day and time, it is her effort and practice to *accomplish it in fantasy*. Everything she does in *reality* too is colored by this necessity, this compulsion to be *special*. So, in fact, *reality becomes fantasy too*. She makes it so!

[...] It [tradition] makes Blanche feel *alone, outside of her society*. Left out, insecure, shaky. The airs the "tradition" demands isolate her further, and every once in a while, her resistance weakened by drink, she breaks down and seeks human warmth and contact where she can find it, not on her terms, on theirs; the merchant, the traveling salesman and the others ... among whom the vulgar adolescent soldiers seem the most innocent. [...] That [protection] is what she, as a woman in the tradition, so desperately needs. That's what she comes to Stella for, Stella and her husband. Not finding it from them she tries to get it from Mitch. *Protection*. A haven, a *harbor*. She is a refugee, punch drunk, and on the ropes, making her last stand, trying to keep up a gallant front, because she is a proud person. But really if Stella doesn't provide her haven, *where is she to go*. She's a misfit, a liar, her "airs" alienate people, she must act superior to them which alienates them further. [...]

Stanley, whom she's antagonized by her destructiveness aimed at his home, but especially by her need to be superior, uses her past, which he digs up, to destroy her. Finally she takes refuge in fantasy. She must have protection, closeness, love, safe harbor. The only place she can obtain them any longer is in her own mind. She "goes crazy."

Stella

Spine – hold onto Stanley (Blanche the antagonist).

One reason Stella submits to Stanley's solution at the end, is perfectly ready to, is that she has an unconscious hostility toward Blanche. Blanche is so patronizing, demanding and superior toward her ... makes her so useless, old-fashioned and helpless ... everything that Stanley has got her out of. Stanley has made a woman out of her. Blanche immediately returns her to the subjugations of childhood, younger-sister-ness.

[...] She's in a sensual stupor. She shuts out all challenge all day long. She loafs, does her hair, her nails, fixes a dress, doesn't eat much, but prepares Stanley's dinner and waits for Stanley. She hopes for no other meaning from life. Her pregnancy just makes it more so.

[...] Stella is doomed too. She has sold herself out for a temporary solution. She's given up all hope, everything, just to live for Stanley's pleasures. [...] She is Stanley's slave. She has sold out most of her life. Latent in Stella is rebellion. Blanche arouses it. [...] At the end of the play, her life is entirely different. It will never be the same with Stanley again.

Note from Tennessee Williams on the fourth day of rehearsal: "Gadge [Elia Kazan's nickname] – I am a bit concerned over Stella in Scene One. It seems to me that she has too much vivacity [...]. Blanche is the quick, light one. Stella is relatively slow and almost indolent. Blanche mentions her 'Chinese philosophy' – the way she sits with her little hands folded like a cherub in a choir, etc. I think her natural passivity is one of the things that makes her acceptance of Stanley acceptable. She naturally 'gives in', accepts, lets things slide, she does not make much of an effort."

Stanley

Spine – keep things his way (Blanche the antagonist).

The hedonist [...]. He has all the confidence of resurgent flesh. Also with a kind of naïveté ... even slowness ... he means no harm. He wants to knock no one down. He only doesn't want to be taken advantage of. His code is simple and simple-minded. [...]

But what is the chink in his armor now, the contradiction? Why does Blanche get so completely under his skin? Why does he want to bring Blanche and, before her, Stella *down to his level*? It's as if he said: "I know I haven't got much, but no one has more and no one's going to have more." It's the hoodlum aristocrat. He's deeply dissatisfied, deeply hopeless, deeply cynical ... the physical immediate pleasures , if they come in a steady enough stream quiet this *as long as no one gets more* ... then his bitterness comes forth and he tears down the pretender. But Blanche he can't seem to do anything with. She can't come down to his level so he levels her with his sex. He brings her right down to his level, beneath him.

One of the important things for Stanley is that Blanche *would wreck his home*. Blanche is dangerous. She is destructive. She would soon have him and Stella fighting. He's got things the way he wants them around there and he does *not* want them upset by a phony, corrupt, sick, destructive woman. *This makes Stanley right!* Are we going into the era of Stanley? He may be practical and right ... but what the hell does it leave us? [...]

Emphasize Stanley's love for Stella. It is rough, embarrassed and he rather truculently *won't show it*. [...]

Stanley is supremely indifferent to everything except his own pleasure and comfort. He is marvelously selfish, a miracle of sensuous self-centeredness. He builds a hedonist life, and fights to the death to defend it – but finally it is *not* enough to hold Stella *and* this philosophy is not successful even for him – because every once in a while the silenced, frustrated part of Stanley breaks loose in unexpected and unpredictable ways and we suddenly see, as in a burst of lightning, his real frustrated self. Usually his frustration is worked off by eating a lot, drinking a lot, gambling a lot, fornicating a lot. He's going to get very far later. He's desperately trying to squeeze out happiness by living by *ball and jowl* ... and it really doesn't work ... because it simply stores up violence and stores up violence, until every *bar in the nation is full of Stanley to explode*. He's desperately trying to drug his senses ... overwhelming them with a constant round of sensation so that he will feel nothing else.

In Stanley sex goes under a disguise. Nothing is more erotic and arousing to him than "airs" ... she thinks she's better than me ... I'll show her. [...] Sex equals domination ... anything that challenges him – like calling him "common" – arouses him sexually.

[...]

As a character Stanley is most interesting in his "contradictions", his "soft" moments, his sudden pathetic little-tough-boy tenderness toward Stella. Scene 3 he cries like a baby. Somewhere in Scene 8 he almost makes it up with Blanche. In Scene 10 he *does* try to make it up with her –and except for her doing the one thing that most arouses him, both in anger and sex, he might have.

Mitch

Spine – get away from his mother (Blanche the lever).

He wants the perfection his mother gave him ... everything is approving, protective, *perfect for him*. Naturally no girl, today, no sensible, decent girl will give him this. But the tradition will.

Like Stella, Mitch hides from his own problem through mother-love.

Mitch is the end product of a matriarchy ... his mother has robbed him of all daring, initiative, self-reliance. He does not face his own needs.

[...] He is big, tough, burly, has a rough southern voice and a manner of homespun, coarse, awkward, overgrown boy, with a heart of mush. [...]

Mitch, too, is most interesting in his basic contradictions. He doesn't want to be Mother's Boy. Goddamn it he just can't help it. He does love his Mother, but is a little embarrassed at how much. Blanche makes a man out of him, makes him important and grown-up. His Mother – he dimly realizes – keeps him eternally adolescent, forever dependent. [...] the reason he's so clumsy with women is that he's so damn full of violent desire for them. [...]

This play contains the crucial struggle of Mitch's life. For Mitch instinctively and even consciously, to a degree, knows what's wrong with him. He is jibed at often enough. And in his guts he knows they're right. Mitch, in his guts, hates his Mother. He loves her in a way – partially out of *early habit*, partially because she is clever – but much more fundamentally he *hates* her. It is a tragedy for him when he returns to her absolute sovereignty at the end. He will never meet another woman who will need him as much as Blanche and will need him to be a man as much as Blanche.

V The Film Version and Other Adaptations of the Play

1. The Film Version

1.1 The production of the film and its problems

According to Palmer ("Hollywood in crisis: Tennessee Williams and the evolution of the adult film", p. 205), "Williams's work strongly influenced the development of the film industry itself. [...] To my knowledge, no other author through his works alone has had this kind of influence on the history of a national cinema. From this point of view, seven of the fifteen films based on Williams's work are of major importance: *The Glass Menagerie* (1950), *A Streetcar Named Desire* (1951), *The Rose Tattoo* (1955), *Baby Doll* (1956), *The Fugitive Kind* (1960), *Cat on a Hot Tin Roof* (1958), and *Sweet Bird of Youth* (1962)."
In the 1950s audiences began to dislike Hollywood films with happy endings and flat characters and became more interested in tragic themes, multi-layered characters and modern cinematic effects. Instead of the productions of the Hollywood film industry of "clean, wholesome entertainment conforming to a detailed series of protocols – the Production Code," the film versions of Tennessee Williams' plays constituted the so-called "adult film" with psychologically complex characters who are confronted with sexual conflicts, homosexuality, drug addiction, etc., all of them themes that were not allowed to be dealt with or even alluded to because of the censorship of the Production Code Administration (PCA) that had been founded by the film producers in 1934 in response to Catholic demands (cf. Palmer, pp. 207 f).
As the censors demanded that films should be produced to promote the traditional American middle-class values and clearly differentiate between the good and the evil, Tennessee Williams' plays such as *A Streetcar Named Desire* did not correspond to the principles of the Production Code because they presented complex characters and conflicts that appealed to the viewers emotionally and also challenged them to reflect on the moral problems without being offered a black-and-white solution. Thus the playwright, the producer and the director were asked to change scenes and eliminate morally offensive subjects such as the reference to Allan's homosexuality (cf. Palmer, p. 208). But they were restored in the 1993 version of the film and its home video release:

- Stella mentions that she was thrilled by Stanley's smashing the light bulbs on their wedding night.
- Allan's homosexuality is alluded to.
- Blanche expresses that she wishes to kiss the young collector "on the mouth".
- When Stella returns to her husband after he has beaten her, her face is shown in a close-up blank with desire.
- Before he rapes Blanche Stanley's says: "Maybe you wouldn't be so bad to interfere with."

After the great success of the play and the winning of the Pulitzer Prize in 1947, Hollywood film producers were not interested in producing a film version of the play for two years because of the restrictive Production Code. Elia Kazan considered making the film without a Production Code certificate in cooperation with the independent film company of Charles Feldman, who had bought the screen rights. But as Warner Brothers insisted on the approval of the Production Code Administration before the film was produced in their studio, Tennessee Williams and Elia Kazan agreed to change two aspects of the play because of the censors' objections: Blanche's young husband was no longer homosexual but possibly impotent and Blanche's "nymphomania" was less obvious. But Williams and Kazan refused to cut Blanche's rape and justified it as essential for the whole play (cf. Williams' Letter to Breen in Chapter VI, 5.4). Breen agreed on condition that at the end of the film Stella no longer trusts her husband (cf. Palmer, pp. 215 ff). She does not allow Stanley to touch her but takes her baby in her arms and runs upstairs to Eunice. Tennessee Williams had to accept that the ending was "softened up" but underlined that it is "a total contradiction to the meaning of the play", when Stanley and Stella go on living together (cf. *Conversations*, p. 275).
Due to marketing requirements Warner Brothers insisted on replacing Jessica Tandy, who had successfully played the role of Blanche in New York, by Vivien Leigh, who in 1939 had become famous for her role of the Southern belle Scarlett O'Hara in the commercially extremely successful film version of Margaret Mitchell's novel *Gone with the Wind*. Tennessee Williams admired Vivien Leigh because she is "incomparably graceful, she moves like a marvelous dancer, on or off stage, and she has an instinct for doing and saying just the one right thing [...] she is not only a stunning actress but a lady with the most important part of that intricate composition, which is kindness of heart." (*Essays*, pp. 127 f)
The other three major characters were played by the same actors as in the stage production, i.e. Marlon Brando as Stanley, Kim Hunter as Stella and Karl Malden as Mitch. Tennessee Williams believed that Marlon Brando was "America's most gifted actor" (*Essays*, p. 129) and the ideal Stanley because of the intensity of his playing the role and his physical attraction. When the

film was released in 1951 it was highly praised by critics, a great commercial success and awarded four Oscars, namely for the leading role of Vivien Leigh, for Kim Hunter and Karl Malden as supporting players and for Best Art Direction-Set decoration, Black-and-White. As the film had got 12 nominations and Marlon Brando (despite his extraordinarily impressive presentation of Stanley), Williams and Kazan were not rewarded but instead the musical film *An American in Paris* (1951) as Best Picture, they were rather disappointed. But Elia Kazan won the New York Film Critics Circle Award (Best Director and Best Film) and the Special Jury Prize at Venice Film Festival (http://www.imdb.com/title/tt0044081/awards).

1.2 Film analysis

The following film analysis refers to the DVD distributed by Warner Home Video, 2006, which presents the film based on the screenplay by Oscar Saul and directed by Elia Kazan. This adaptation of the play does not contain the reference to Allan Grey's homosexuality and has a different ending, since Stella refuses to be comforted by her husband and does not want to return to him.

The black-and-white film begins in the conventional way with the logo of Warner Bros. Pictures and the film title: "The Pulitzer Prize and New York Critics Award Play 'A Streetcar named Desire'. An Elia Kazan Production" followed by the opening credits of the names of the producer Charles K. Feldman, the director Elia Kazan, the cast: Vivien Leigh, Marlon Brando, Karl Malden, Kim Hunter and others, the scriptwriter Oscar Saul, the cinematographer Harry Stradling, the composer Alex North and others. In the background of the opening credits the house is shown where Blanche wants to stay with her sister and a Jazz band can be heard.

Before the action begins New Orleans is presented by an establishing long shot from the bird's eye. A train approaches the station in the dusk and taxis are driving in the street obviously to pick up the passengers. In the station a bride and groom followed by their wedding guests happily pass by in the background before Blanche appears out of the steam of the engine. While lots of passengers walk to the exit behind her, she is shown in a medium shot looking at a piece of paper and uncertain where to go. A sailor asks to help her and accompanies her to the tram, which just arrives. Its name Desire is shown in a close-up.

Thus Elia Kazan deviates from the stage production but makes use of cinematic means to convey the impression that Blanche feels lost and needs the help of a stranger to get into the right tram. The wedding group seems to foreshadow her desire to marry.

Before Blanche meets Eunice in front of her house, the night life in a street in the French Quarter is shown with bars where Jazz is played. Contrary to

the play Blanche meets her sister at the bowling alley where they rapturously embrace each other. Blanche sees Stanley the first time and is shocked because he is shown as a strong man quarrelling with other bowlers and is admired by his wife.
After a cut Blanche and Stella are shown in the apartment. Their talk is presented by over-the-shoulder shots and reverse-angle shots, which are used throughout the film when the characters talk to each other. During the talk Blanche is smoking and drinking. As in the play she is characterized as talkative, nervous and displeased with the narrow apartment. When she tells about Belle Reve and accuses her sister her emotions are expressed by her facial play which is shown in a close-up. This kind of shot is frequently used in the film to stress the characters' feelings. As Elia Kazan concentrates on the talk, several actions of the stage production such as Blanche's looking for the whisky bottle are left out. Contrary to the play the noise of a train underlines Blanche's "hysterical" description of her life at Belle Reve.
When Stella is deeply hurt by Blanche's words and runs to the bathroom, the noisy arrival of Stanley and his friends and the angry shouting of Eunice upstairs are shown. Blanche first hides behind the curtain when she sees Stanley whose strong build is underlined by a medium shot. Their talk corresponds to the play apart from the name of Laurel which in the film is Auriol. During the talk their different height and Stanley's self-confidence versus Blanche's insecurity is shown when the camera tilts up or down. Stanley is chewing and looks superior whereas Blanche behaves nervously and is frightened when a cat suddenly screeches. She instinctively touches Stanley's arm as if looking for help and is irritated when Stanley calmly looks at her and starts laughing. When Stanley refers to her marriage, the word "married" is echoed and Blanche's face is shown in a close-up. She looks terrified and is obviously reminded of her husband's suicide since the polka tune is heard and the gunshot, which ends her hallucination. At the end of the scene she nearly faints.
Contrary to the play the street in front of Stella's home is shown and the shout "Fresh fish!" can be heard. A convertible driven by Stanley is shown in a medium long shot with Blanche's trunk in the boot. Stanley and Steve carry the trunk to the apartment. After a cut Stella asks her husband to be nice to Blanche and kisses him while Stanley is eating and seems to agree. After that the action is similar to the play when Stanley wants to see the papers about the loss of Belle Reve, gets angry, tears the clothes and the jewellery out of Blanche's trunk and intends to ask experts he knows about their real value.
Stella is upset about her husband's rude behaviour and puts the clothes back. Blanche leaves the bathroom, looks at her clothes and tries to flirt with Stanley. She is upset and cries when Allan's love letters fall to the floor, throws the documents of the plantation on a table and Stanley decides to have them checked.

The controversy between Stanley and Blanche is mainly shown by medium shots and over-the-shoulder shots. Blues music can be heard. When Stanley tells Blanche that Stella is pregnant, Blanche's sad face is shown in a mirror. When Stella and Blanche leave for a night out a vendor of hot dogs and not tamale as in the play passes the apartment and shouts: "Red hots!"
After a cut and contrary to the play Eunice is shown in bed. She gets up and is angry because the poker play has not yet finished. The players are shown drinking and smoking when Stella and Blanche return from their night out. Stanley who treats his partners rudely hits Stella on the bottom, which makes her angry. As in the play Blanche meets Mitch in front of the bathroom and they have a polite talk. He returns to the poker table but cannot concentrate on the play while Stella and Blanche fool around in the bedroom. Stanley gets angry and turns the radio off though Blanche wants to listen to rumba music. Mitch is angry about Stanley's behaviour and goes to Blanche. They talk about the silver case. The camera tilts down to show Blanche sitting and it tilts up when Mitch fastens the lantern around the bulb. This camera movement is frequently used to show their different height. Their talk is accompanied by soft music and suddenly interrupted by the furious shouts of Stanley which are angrily answered by Mitch to underline that he is more interested in Blanche than playing poker. Blanche turns the radio on again and fascinates Mitch when she dances a waltz whose words *Wien, Wien, nur du allein sollst die Stadt meiner Träume sein* seem to underline her living in a dream world. Stanley throws the radio through a window, pushes his wife to the veranda and beats her outside the room. A brutal brawl starts until Mitch, Steve and Pablo force Stanley under the shower and then run home.
Stanley seems to be sober again and is shown weeping. It is said that Marlon Brando shed real tears. After ringing up Eunice and desperately shouting Stella's name, the camera tilts up to show Eunice on top of the stairs and then alternately shows Stella slowly and seductively coming down the stairs and Stanley waiting downstairs until he falls to his knees. They passionately embrace each other and Stella is carried to the bedroom. Blanche is upset and rushes down the staircase, meets Mitch and tells him that she needs kindness now.
The action of Act Four and Act Five corresponds to the stage performance. But whereas in the play "a murmur of thunder" can be heard, there is a thunderstorm in the film. When Blanche tells that she must be attractive violin music can be heard in the background. Stella and Blanche are alternately shown in a close-up when Blanche tells her sister that she intends to deceive Mitch into marriage and Stella encourages her.
While Stanley is shown outside in good spirits, Blanche is depressed and sitting on a chair. The cathedral chimes and soft music can be heard. When the young collector appears, Blanche seems to be reminded of the seventeen-year-old student in Laurel. She begins to flirt with him in the same way as

with Mitch by asking him if he has got a light. Medium shots and over-the-shoulder shots present Blanche and the young collector during the talk. Blanche calls him back several times when he wants to leave, romantically imagines that he is a prince and finally kisses him on the mouth, which is shown in a close-up. The collector is bewildered and runs away whereas like in the play Blanche remembers that she must "keep her hands off children." When Mitch appears with a bunch of flowers Blanche calls him her "Rosenkavalier" and asks him to bow whereas she curtseys to him.

There is a jump-cut and contrary to Scene Six of the play where Mitch and Blanche return from the amusement park on Lake Pontchartrain they are shown dancing in a dance hall while a Jazz band is playing loudly. Blanche and Mitch leave the dance floor and have a nightcap outside on the terrace where Blanche lights a candle and pours beer into the glasses. Their talk and action is nearly the same as in Scene Six. When she tells about Allan, she stands at the railings looking towards the misty lake. Allan was her first love and she adored him. But contrary to the play she does not mention that he was homosexual but that she could not understand him since he was soft, wrote poems and could not find a job. One night he was crying like a child. When she tells how he committed suicide, she is deeply moved and says: "I killed him" and instead of the noise of a steam engine a shot is heard, which signals the end of her nightmare. The camera tilts down on them when Mitch embraces and kisses her.

Whereas the following short scene differs from the play since Stanley and Mitch are shown quarrelling in the factory building, Scene Seven and Eight correspond to the talk and action in the stage performance to a large extent. The positions, angles and movements of the camera mentioned above are the same in order to present the characters talk, emotions and actions.

When Blanche is sitting alone in the dark her depressive mood is shown in a close-up. A blues can be heard in the background. Suddenly Mitch violently knocks on the door and wants to see her, which makes her hectically run around, trying to dress up and putting her make-up on. As Mitch has to wait, he gets furious, kicks down the door and behaves rudely to Blanche who is confused and seems to be mentally disturbed. When she hears the polka tune and the shot, Mitch asks her if she is mad. Blanche tries to calm him and in vain offers him a glass of "Southern Cheer", which possibly replaces "Southern Comfort" of the play to prevent product placement. As Mitch wants to see her face, he tears down the lantern from the bulb and keeps Blanche's face under the lamp.

Her face is shown in a close-up which reveals that she looks frightened and rather old. When she is pushed down on an armchair, Blanche honestly describes her promiscuous past life while Mitch turns his back towards her. The Mexican woman selling flowers for the dead appears at the door and frightens Blanche who then tells Mitch about her dying relatives and her desire for young soldiers. Mitch kisses her but refuses to marry her since she is not "clean" enough and flees out of the apartment when Blanche starts screaming, which is stressed by a shrill piece of music. People in the street look at her and want to know what the matter is. But she retreats into the apartment and shuts all the windows. When a policeman knocks on the door and asks her if she is all right, she answers "Yes".

Blanche is shown in an extravagant dress with the tiara on and is talking to herself, which conveys the impression that she can no longer distinguish between illusion and reality. She seems to live in a dream world. When Stanley arrives good-humoured, the following talk and action correspond to Scene Ten of the play except that Blanche is thrown onto the bed by Stanley and the camera tilts down to show her fright in a close-up. She panics and as if insane snatches up her clothes in order to flee. But when the Mexican woman appears out of the fog and offers her flowers for the dead, Blanche is horrified and says: "Not now!" She rushes to the telephone and in vain cries for help. Like in the scene before her birthday cake is shown on the table. It has not been touched and the candles are out, which seems to symbolize her tragic end. The following action is the same as in the play when Blanche in vain tries to defend herself with the neck of a broken bottle and Stanley circles round her as if she were his prey. The scene is mainly presented in a reverse-angle shot. Contrary to the play Stanley does not carry her to the bed but subdues her and Blanche's horrified face is shown in a broken mirror.

Unlike Scene Eleven of the play the following scene begins with the cleaning of the street in front of the apartment. Then the baby in a pram is shown. At the poker table Stanley tells that Blanche is mixed up in her mind and Blanche looks distraught when she leaves the bathroom. Stella has a guilty conscience but hypocritically talks to Blanche in a friendly way. The cathedral bells chime and after a cut the Doctor and the Matron arrive, which makes Blanche panic. The words Stanley and the Matron say echo in Blanche's mind and contribute to the impression that she is totally distraught or insane. She tries to flee. When Stanley gives her the lantern, Mitch gives him a right hook to the jaw and Steve and Pablo are hostile towards Stanley. The Matron forces Blanche down to the floor and after a cut the camera tilts down on Blanche who lies helpless on the floor. The Doctor helps her up and leads her out of the apartment before they drive off in a car while Stella despairs and – contrary to the play – does not want to be touched by Stanley. Instead, she takes her crying baby on her arm and runs upstairs to Eunice's apartment without caring for her husband who shouts her name. But Stella's last words are "Never going back. Never!"

At the end of the film the house is shown as at the beginning of the film. The credits are accompanied by blues music.

1.3 Differences between the play and its film version

Elia Kazan transmuted the stage production of *A Streetcar Named Desire* authentically into a film. The author's intention and the main action of the play and the screenplay do not differ. Also the cast is the same apart from Vivien Leigh as Blanche. But the film as a different medium enabled Kazan to include settings and means that cannot be applied for the stage but are essential elements of a cinematic adaptation of a play. This could be elucidated by numerous examples. Here some of the differences shall be described.

When Oscar Saul adapted the play for the screen, he made use of reduction and expansion. For example, he left out the episode when Stanley throws a package of meat up to Stella at the beginning of the play though it is meant to describe his uncivilized behaviour symbolically. Moreover, part of the talk of Blanche and Mitch for instance in Scene Three is left out. Blanche's description of her young husband in Scene Six is shortened. The same applies to Scene Four and also to Scene Eight when Blanche does not finish the parrot story. On the other hand the scriptwriter adds an episode in Stanley's factory, which precedes Scene Seven. Why "Laurel" is replaced by "Auriol" is not evident, possibly the town council was against it.

Instead of the playwright's rather differentiated stage directions which also describe New Orleans and the French Quarter, Kazan presents the panorama of the city in a high-angle long shot and uses on-location shots of the station, the taxis in the street and a wedding group at the beginning of the film. In the play Blanche and Mitch return from the amusement park, whereas in the film they are dancing in a dance hall and have a nightcap on the terrace. Later the night life in the French Quarter, bars where Jazz is played, streets, cars and many people enjoying a night out or watching Blanche scream are shown. It is not always possible to recognize to what extent these scenes are shot in the studio.

There are also long shots for instance to show the station and full shots or medium shots to present people and props. Frequently the camera tilts up or down when the characters walk up or down the staircase. Over-the-shoulder shots or reverse-angle shots are usually used to show the characters talking, arguing or quarrelling, for instance when Blanche and Stanley talk about the loss of Belle Reve.

As it is a black-and-white film, the colours mentioned by Tennessee Williams in his stage directions cannot be shown though they are meant to stress the atmosphere of New Orleans and to symbolize the characters' traits and behaviour. The viewer has to imagine the colours but he can also concentrate more on the action and the problems presented in the film. Contrary to modern films the characters are frequently shown smoking since in a black-and-white film the smoke can be seen better and contributes to the atmosphere of the poker night for instance.

Whereas the distance between the stage and the audience remains the same, in the film there are variations between camera and object. Thus in Kazan's film New Orleans is shown in an extreme long shot from above whereas Blanche's emotions are shown in close-ups. Contrary to the stage performance her face can be seen in an oval mirror several times throughout the film showing her vanity or sorrowful face in a close-up whereas in the play she looks at herself in the mirror of the dressing-table several times without the audience being able to see her face closely. Finally her horrified face can be seen in the broken mirror when she is raped by Stanley, which has a more dramatic effect than the use of the hand mirror at the beginning of Scene Ten in the play where she slams it down that the glass cracks since she dislikes her looks. Nevertheless, both in the play and the film the symbolic use of the mirror and the lantern is emphasized. Also the appearance of the Mexican woman who sells flowers for the dead has a strong dramatic effect in the film because Blanche is shocked when she is offered the flowers at the door. In the play the Mexican woman "is only faintly visible outside the building" (p. 90, ll. 35 f) and reminds Blanche of her dead relatives and the loss of Belle Reve while the mournful cries of the Mexican Woman are heard several times.
The light and sound effects in the play and the film are similar to a certain extent. For instance the polka tune and the shot are heard and also the chime of the cathedral bells. On the other hand the sounds differ, e.g. the score which was composed by Alex North to reflect the mood or the emotions of the characters.

2. Other Adaptations of the Play

Apart from many stage productions of *A Streetcar Named Desire,* there are several TV versions of the play such as the multi-Emmy Award-winning television version of 1984 and the TV version of 1995 starring Jessica Lange, who won a Golden Globe award for her performance of Blanche.
In 1952 a ballet production was staged in Montreal. The music was composed by Alex North, who also composed the music for the film version of the play.
In 1995 André Previn composed an opera based on the play with the libretto written by Philip Littell. Its premiere was at San Francisco Opera during the 1998 season.
In the *New York Times* review of 21 September 1998 Bernard Holland wrote: "*A Streetcar Named Desire* is so operatic as a play that one wonders why more than 50 years passed since its Broadway opening with no opera of note being made of it. [...] First of all, it sings very well. Mr. Previn has a fine ear for voices. He knows how to flatter and coax it and send it gracefully from one musical episode to the next [...] one had the impression that Mr. Previn had

been writing for the musical theater all his life. [...] There are angry clashes of harmony and key, many Straussian gestures, sweet-as-honey popular melody and the kinds of corporate noodling and mumbling among the strings native to a Ligeti or a Penderecki. Mr. Previn is not ashamed to incorporate Hollywood code words, especially the wailing thrusts of saxophone, trumpet and clarinet to introduce dissolution and lurid sex."
In the following years the opera was performed in several cities in the United States, Europe, Japan and Australia.

A Streetcar Named Marge is a musical version of the play in the American animated series "The Simpsons" but received negative feedback since it totally missed the point of Tennessee Williams' play. There are several references to the playwright in rock songs. (http://en.wikipedia.org/wiki/Tennessee_Williams)

Apart from referring to the playwright in book titles, Donald Spoto refers to Blanche's final statement when he chose it as the title of his biography of Tennessee Williams: *The Kindness of Strangers* (1997).

VI Additional Materials

The additional materials offer some background information about Tennessee Williams' views of his work and his way of writing. The following texts refer to several ideas and topics the playwright dealt with in *A Streetcar Named Desire*.
You could also make use of the materials when you analyze the play or wish to comment on the dramatist's views. The additional texts could also help to write an essay or term paper about *A Streetcar Named Desire* or one of its topics and problems you consider important.
Some of the playwright's ideas could also inspire you to read or see another play Tennessee Williams has written or to watch and analyze its film adaptation.

1. Tennessee Williams on his Work and his Way of Writing

1.1 Memoirs

In his *Memoirs* Tennessee Williams describes what writing means to him, how he used to work every day and why he did not like to write about his plays.

> "Maybe I am a machine, a typist. A compulsive typist and a compulsive writer. But that's my life, and what is in these memoirs is mostly the barest periphery of that which is my intense life, for my intense life is my work." (pp. 84 f)
> "What is it like being a writer? I would say it is like being free.
> I know that some writers aren't free, they are professionally employed which is quite a different thing.
> Professionally, they are probably better writers in the conventional sense of "better." They have an ear to the ground of best-seller demands: they please their publishers and presumably their public as well.
> But they are not free and so they are not what I regard a true writer as being.
> To be free is to have achieved your life.
> It means any number of freedoms.
> It means the freedom to stop when you please, to go where and when you please, it means to be voyager here and there, one who flees many hotels, sad or happy, without obstruction and without much regret.
> It means the freedom of being. And someone has wisely observed, if you can't be yourself, what's the point of being anything at all?" (p. 230)

"Why do I resist writing about my plays? The truth is that my plays have been the most important element of my life for God knows how many years. But I feel the plays speak for themselves. And that my life hasn't and that it has been remarkable enough, in its continual contest with madness, to be worth setting upon paper. And my habits of work are so much more private than my daily and nightly existence." (pp. 153 f)

"Well, now, about my plays, what about them? Plays are written and then, if they are lucky, they are performed, and if their luck still holds, which is not too frequently the case, their performance is so successful that both audience and critics at the first night are aware that they are being offered a dramatic work which is both honest and entertaining and also somehow capable of engaging their aesthetic appreciation.
I have never liked to talk about the professional side of my life. Am I afraid that it is a bird that will be startled away by discussion, as by a hawk's shadow? Something like that, I suppose.
People are always asking me, at those symposia to which I've been subjected in recent years, which is my favorite among the plays I have written, the number of which eludes my recollection, and I either say to them, 'Always the latest' or succumb to my instinct for the truth and say, 'I suppose it must be the published version of *Cat on a Hot Tin Roof.*'
That play comes closest to being both a work of art and a work of craft. It is really well put together, in my opinion, and all its characters are amusing and credible and touching. And it adheres to the valuable edict of Aristotle that a

> tragedy must have unity of time and place and magnitude of theme.
> The set in *Cat* never changes and its running time is exactly the time of its action, meaning that one act, timewise, follows directly upon the other, and I know of no other modern American play in which this is accomplished.
> However my reasons for liking *Cat* best are deeper than that. I believe that in *Cat* I reached beyond myself, in the second act, to a kind of crude eloquence of expressions in Big Daddy that I have managed to give to no other character of my creation." (p. 168)

Tennessee Williams considers the published version of *Cat on a Hot Tin Roof* (1954) as his best play and not its stage production because of the changes he was asked by Elia Kazan to realize in order to "improve" the play's "faults". But the opening of the play in New York was "dreadful" and "a failure" as he thought because it was "a "distortion" of what he intended (p. 169). As he experienced a writer's block, he began to take artificial stimulants to start writing again:

> "Since the summer of 1955 I have written usually under artificial stimulants, aside from the true stimulant of my deep-rooted need to continue to write.
> I could cross the room to a big bag containing my collected works – as collected and published this year by New Directions – and provide you with the list of plays I have written since that summer and I think it would make you wonder a bit at my ability to continue my work under these debauched conditions.
> Of course I could cite a number of known artists, I mean writing ones, who also succumbed to artificial stimulants. I could mention Faulkner's practice of climbing into the loft of a barn on his Mississippi farm with a full bottle of bourbon when he was intending to write, which I assume was each morning.
> And I could cite Coleridge and I could mention Jean Cocteau, all of whose best writing was done under opium, I have heard on good authority.
> I could mention many productive and honest writers who went the way of liquor, especially in middle years.
> Yet I would, of course, not advise any young writer to elect that way until it is forced upon him, until he cannot continue his work without resorting to stimulants." (p. 171)

Considering his declining success after 1962 in the Foreword of his *Memoirs* (pp. xvii ff), Tennessee Williams reflects on his goal of writing, his career and the kind of theatre he would like to write for:

> "The truth is that I don't know whether or not I can ever again receive a persuasively favorable critical response to my theatre work in this country, I know the answer no more than does the dog.
> But I am not embittered nor even greatly disconcerted by this dilemma in which I find myself. In a way, it does seem that I have almost asked for it. There is a duality in my attitude toward an audience now. Of course I want their approval, I want their understanding and their empathy. But there is much about them that strikes me as obdurately resistant to my kind of theatre these days.

They seem to be conditioned to a kind of theatre which is quite different from the kind I wish to practice.
Actually my own theatre is also in a state of revolution: I am quite through with the kind of play that established my early and popular reputation. I am doing a different thing which is altogether my own, not influenced at all by other playwrights at home or abroad or by other schools of theatre. My thing is what it always was: to express my world and my experience of it in whatever form seems suitable to the material.
Since *The Night of the Iguana*, the circumstances of my life have demanded of me a continually less traditional style of dramatic writing: I am referring to such works as *The Gnädiges Fräulein, In the Bar of a Tokyo Hotel,* and, most recently, the latest production of *Out Cry*. And, to an extent, the style of these memoirs.
[...]
Has any of my writing been 'a professional matter'? I have always written for deeper necessities than the term 'professional' implies, and I think that this has sometimes been to the detriment of my career. But more of the time to its advantage. Career? The wrong word. I should have said – no, nothing so pretentious as 'vocation'. But truly, I never had any choice but to be a writer."

1.2 Tennessee Williams interviews himself

In his Essay *The World I Live In*, which appeared in the London *Observer*, April 7, 1957 (cf. *Essays*, p. 88–92) Tennessee Williams simulates an interview of himself and answers questions he believes are particularly relevant:

Question. Can we talk frankly?
Answer. There's no other way we can talk.

Q. Perhaps you know that when your first successful play, *The Glass Menagerie,* was revived early this season, a majority of the reviewers felt that it was still the best play you have written, although it is now twelve years old?
A. Yes, I read all my play notices and criticisms, even those that say that I write for money and that my primary appeal is to brutal and ugly instincts.

Q. Where there is so much smoke – !
A. A fire smokes the most when you start pouring water on it.

Q. But surely you'll admit that there's been a disturbing note of harshness and coldness and violence and anger in your more recent works?
A. I think, without planning to do so, I have followed the developing tension and anger and violence of the world and time that I live in through my own steadily increasing tension as a writer and person.

Q. Then you admit that this "developing tension," as you call it, is a reflection of a condition in yourself?
A. Yes.

Q. A morbid condition?
A. Yes.

Q. Perhaps verging on the psychotic?
A. I guess my work has always been a kind of psychotherapy for me.

Q. But how can you expect audiences to be impressed by plays and other writings that are created as a release for the tensions of a possible or incipient madman?
A. It releases their own.

Q. Their own what?
A. Increasing tensions, verging on the psychotic.

Q. You think the world's going mad?
A. Going? I'd say nearly gone! As the Gypsy said in *Camino Real,* the world is a funny paper read backwards. And that way it isn't so funny.

Q. How far do you think you can go with this tortured view of the world?
A. As far as the world can go in its tortured condition, maybe that far, but no further.

Q. You don't expect audiences and critics to go along with you, do you?
A. No.

Q. Then why do you push and pull them that way?
A. I go that way. I don't push or pull anyone with me.

Q. Yes, but you hope to continue to have people listen to you, don't you?
A. Naturally I hope to.

Q. Even if you throw them off by the violence and horror of your works?
A. Haven't you noticed that people are dropping all around you, like moths out of the season, as the result of the present plague of violence and horror in this world and time that we live in?

Q. But you're an entertainer, with artistic pretensions, and people are not entertained any more by cats on hot tin roofs and Baby Dolls and passengers on crazy streetcars!
A. Then let them go to the musicals and the comedies. I'm not going to change my ways. It's hard enough for me to write what I want to write without me trying to write what you say they want me to write which I don't want to write.

Q. Do you have any positive message, in your opinion?
A. Indeed I do think that I do.

Q. Such as what?
A. The crying, almost screaming, need of a great worldwide human effort to know ourselves and each other a great deal better, well enough to concede that no man has a monopoly on right or virtue any more than any man has a corner on duplicity and evil and so forth. If people, and races and nations, would start

with that self-manifest truth, then I think that the world could sidestep the sort of corruption which I have involuntarily chosen as the basic, allegorical theme of my plays as a whole.

Q. You sound as if you felt quite detached and superior to this process of corruption in society.
A. I have never written about any kind of vice which I can't observe in myself.

Q. But you accuse society, as a whole, of succumbing to a deliberate mendacity, and you appear to find yourself separate from it as a writer.
A. As a writer, yes, but not as a person.

Q. Do you think this is a peculiar virtue of yours as a writer?
A. I'm not sentimental about writers. But I'm inclined to think that most writers, and most other artists, too, are primarily motivated in their desperate vocation by a desire to find and to separate truth from the complex of lies and evasions they live in, and I think that this impulse is what makes their work not so much a profession as a vocation, a true "calling."

Q. Why don't you write about nice people? Haven't you ever known any nice people in your life?
A. My theory about nice people is so simple that I am embarrassed to say it.

Q. Please say it!
A. Well, I've never met one that I couldn't love if I completely knew him and understood him, and in my work I have at least tried to arrive at knowledge and understanding.
I don't believe in "original sin." I don't believe in "guilt." I don't believe in villains or heroes – only right or wrong ways that individuals have taken, not by choice but by necessity or by certain still-uncomprehended influences in themselves, their circumstances, and their antecedents.
This is so simple I'm ashamed to say it, but I'm sure it's true. In fact, I would bet my life on it! And that's why I don't understand why our propaganda machines are always trying to teach us, to persuade us, to hate and fear other people on the same little world that we live in.
Why don't we meet these people and get to know them as I try to meet and know people in my plays? This sounds terribly vain and egoistical.
I don't want to end on such a note. Then what shall I say? That I know that I am a minor artist who has happened to write one or two major works? I can't even say which they are. It doesn't matter. I have said my say. I may still say it again, or I may shut up now. It doesn't depend on you, it depends entirely on me, and the operation of chance or Providence in my life.

2. Tennessee Williams: *On A Streetcar Named Success*

From: *The New York Times*, Drama Section, November 30, 1947, quoted from: Day, Christine R. and Woods, Bob: *Where I Live. Selected Essays*, pp. 15–22 (extracts).

This essay was published in *The New York Times* four days before the New York opening of *A Streetcar Named Desire*. At the beginning of the essay the playwright describes that his life totally changed after the tremendous success of *The Glass Menagerie* in Chicago. Suddenly he was a wealthy man living on room-service in a luxury hotel. But he disliked it and even became indifferent to people. He suspected his friends of hypocrisy and did not want to see them. The essay continues as follows:

> I got so sick of hearing people say, "I loved your play!" that I could not say thank you any more. I choked on the words and turned rudely away from the usually sincere person. I no longer felt any pride in the play itself but began to dislike it, probably because I felt too lifeless inside ever to create another. I was walking around dead in my shoes and I knew it but there were no friends I knew or trusted sufficiently, at that time, to take them aside and tell them what was the matter.
>
> This curious condition persisted about three months, till late spring, when I decided to have another eye operation mainly because of the excuse it gave me to withdraw from the world behind a gauze mask. [...]
>
> When the gauze mask was removed I found myself in a readjusted world. I checked out of the handsome suite at the first-class hotel, packed my papers and a few incidental belongings, and left for Mexico, an elemental country where you can quickly forget the false dignities and conceits imposed by success, a country where vagrants innocent as children curl up to sleep on the pavements and human voices, especially when their language is not familiar to the ear, are soft as birds'. My public self, that artifice of mirrors, did not exist here and so my natural being was resumed.
>
> Then, as a final act of restoration, I settled for a while at Chapala to work on a play called *The Poker Night*, which later became *A Streetcar Named Desire*. It is only in his work that an artist can find reality and satisfaction, for the actual world is less intense than the world of his invention, and consequently his life, without recourse to violent disorder, does not seem very substantial. The right condition for him is that in which his work is not only convenient but unavoidable.
>
> [...]

This is an oversimplification. One does not escape that easily from the seduction of an effete way of life. You cannot arbitrarily say to yourself, I will now continue my life as it was before this thing, Success, happened to me. But once you fully apprehend the vacuity of a life without struggle you are equipped with the basic means of salvation. Once you know this is true, that the heart of man, his body and his brain, are forged in a white-hot furnace for the purpose of conflict (the struggle of creation) and that with the conflict removed, the man is a sword cutting daisies, that not privation but luxury is the wolf at the door and that the fangs of this wolf are all the little vanities and conceits and laxities that Success is heir to – why, then with this knowledge you are at least in a position of knowing where danger lies.

You know, then, that the public Somebody you are when you "have a name" is a fiction created with mirrors and that the only somebody worth being is the solitary and unseen you that existed from your first breath and which is the sum of your actions and so is constantly in a state of becoming under your own volition – and knowing these things, you can even survive the catastrophe of Success!

[...]

Then what is good? The obsessive interest in human affairs, plus a certain amount of compassion and moral conviction, that first made the experience of living something that must be translated into pigment of music or bodily movement or poetry or prose or anything that's dynamic and expressive – that's what's good for you if you're at all serious in your aims. William Saroyan wrote a great play on this theme, that purity of heart is the one success worth having. "In the time of your life – live!" That time is short and it doesn't return again. It is slipping away while I write this and while you read it, and the monosyllable of the clock is Loss, loss, loss, unless you devote your heart to its opposition.

3. Tennessee Williams on Blanche and Stanley

Though Tennessee Williams frequently stated that he did not intend or like to explain his plays and the characters, he nevertheless did it in his essays (cf. *Where I Live*, 1978) and in several interviews (cf. *Conversations*, 1986). The following quotations could help understand Blanche and also Stanley better or could be compared with one's own interpretation (cf. Chapter VII "Impulses and Model Tasks").

3.1 Tennessee Williams: *Critic Says "Evasion", Writer Says "Mystery"*, 1955 (*Essays*, pp. 70–74; extract pp. 70–72)

Critics complained, sometimes, of ambiguities in *Streetcar*. Certainly there were many divergent ideas of Blanche's character and many widely differing interpretations in the playing of her character among many productions I saw at home and abroad. She was often referred to as a prostitute, often as a dipso [an alcoholic] or a nympho or liar.

The truth about human character in a play, as in life, varies with the variance of experience and viewpoint of those that view it. No two members of an audience ever leave a theater, after viewing a play that deals with any degree of complexity in character, with identical interpretations of the characters dealt with. This is as it should be. I know full well the defenses and rationalizations of beleaguered writers, a defensive species, but I still feel that I deal unsparingly with what I feel is the truth of character. I would never evade it for the sake of evasion, because I was in any way reluctant to reveal what I know of the truth.

[...]

Some mystery should be left in the revelation of character in a play, just as a great deal of mystery is always left in the revelation of character in life, even in one's own character to himself. This does not absolve the playwright of his duty to observe and probe as clearly and deeply as he *legitimately* can: but it should steer him away from "pat" conclusions, facile definitions, which make a play just a play, not a snare for the truth of human experience.

This, I believe, states clearly my defense of these so-called ambiguities of character in my plays. The point is, of course, arguable. You may prefer to be told precisely what to believe about every character in a play; you may prefer to know precisely what will be the future course of their lives, happy or disastrous or anywhere in between.

Then I am not your playwright. My characters make my play. I always start with them, they take spirit and body in my mind. Nothing that they say or do is arbitrary or invented. They build the play about them like spiders weaving their webs, sea creatures making their shells. I live with them for a year and a half or two years and I know them far better than I know myself, since I created them and not myself.

But still they must have that quality of life which is shadowy. Was Blanche Dubois a liar? She told many lies in the course of *Streetcar* and yet at heart she was truthful.

3.2 Louis Davis: "That Baby Doll Man: Part I", 1957 (*Conversations*, pp. 43–49; extract p. 45)

"Blanche DuBois had a natural elegance, a love of the beautiful, a romantic attitude towards life," Williams said. "My main theme is a defense of that attitude, a violent protest against those things that defeat it."

3.3 Edward R. Murrow: "Interview with Tennessee Williams, Yukio Mishima, and Dilys Powell", 1960 (*Conversations*, pp. 69–77, extract p. 71)

"I thought Blanche – when she rose from the floor because she saw kindness in the eyes of the stranger and walked off with him, taking his arm, to a madhouse, saying "I have always depended on the kindness of strangers" – shows that quality of gallantry which I think is the flag, the great banner, of the human race."

3.4 Studs Terkel Talks with Tennessee Williams, 1961 (*Conversations*, pp. 78–96; extract p. 81)

TW: I think people always find kindness.

ST (Studs Terkel): Well, did Blanche find it as that man took her away?

TW: I think even in asylums one can find kindness if one is willing to give it.

ST: You're asking Blanche to give after the play ends in a sense, aren't you? Blanche is taken –

TW: I have no idea what happens to Blanche after the play ends. I know she was shattered. And the meaning of the play is that this woman who was potentially a superior person was broken by –

ST: Brutality?

TW: Was broken by society.

ST: Society?

TW: The falsities in it.

3.5 John Gruen: "Tennessee Williams. Interview", 1965 (*Conversations*, pp. 112–123; extracts pp. 116 f and pp. 118 f)

Interviewer: To what extent are your plays autobiographical?

Williams: All creative work is autobiographical.

Interviewer: You have created a most provocative gallery of female characters – like Blanche DuBois to the Gnädiges Fräulein. Have you an *idée fixe* regarding women, and Southern women in particular?

Williams: I don't know why I find it much easier, much more interesting to write about women. My sister and my mother were both very articulate women. They talked with great charm. In most of my writings I try to recapture the charm of the way they talked.

Interviewer: Many of your women have a streak in them either of violence or of great vulnerability – such as Blanche DuBois – often a layer of refinement underneath, which, in many cases, is a broken spirit.

Williams: I never find broken spirits in women I admire. My sister, as everyone knows by this time, is a mental invalid, afflicted with schizophrenia. I can say this because she would never hear it. But her spirit is much stronger than my spirit. Nobody who tried to put her down could possibly put her down.

Interviewer: Your male characters, on the other hand, seem marked with characteristics that suggest either a kind of ruggedness, à la Stan Kowalski, or weakness, like Brick [in *Cat on a Hot Tin Roof*]?

Williams: I'm afraid I don't identify very easily with these Stanley Kowalskis and so forth. Maybe I should. They are a sort of mystery to me.

[...]

Interviewer: In reading each of your plays, one detects that the strong are ultimately the most vulnerable, and the weak turn out to have the greater strength and endurance. Is this your observation of life in general?

Williams: I think the weak – if they are not just pusillanimous – are compelled to have more strength than those who are overtly strong. They wouldn't survive at all unless they had this inner strength. They may suffer a great deal for it – and I suppose they do. But I've always felt that Blanche was stronger than Stanley Kowalski.

3.6 Don Lee Keith: "New Tennessee Williams Rises from 'Stoned Age'," 1970 (*Conversations*, pp. 147–160; extract p. 154)

"But I'll be the first to recognize the similarities between my sister and Blanche. In her transition to St. Louis, removed from security and thrown into a world of alarm and despair, Rose had hideous inner turmoil in trying to cope with life. She was fragile and sensitive, and she couldn't cope. Blanche, also fragile and sensitive, couldn't cope either."

3.7 C. Robert Jennings: "Playboy Interview: Tennessee Williams", 1973 (*Conversations*, pp. 224–250; extract p. 244)

Playboy: It's been said that you had an extremely hard time writing *Streetcar*, that it "possessed" you.

Williams: I worked on it on and off for three years or more. I thought it was too big for the theater. Its subjects had not been dealt with before. It was Blanche, this lascivious, demonic woman, who possessed me. *Streetcar* contained just about everything but sadism – which is about the only form of sex of which I disapprove. Cruelty may be the only sin. The rape of Blanche was not sadistic, however, but a natural male retaliation. Stanley said of Blanche, "We've had this date with each other from the beginning!" and he meant it. He had to prove his dominance over this woman in the only way he knew how.

3.8 Cecil Brown: "Interview with Tennessee Williams", 1974 (*Conversations*, pp. 251–283; extract pp. 276 f)

Int.: Is Blanche mad or does she just give in to the situation of her being mad?

Williams: I think she's broken at the end.

Int.: Which is not the same thing?

Williams: She had personal, great strength and personal vulnerability that was finally broken.

Int.: The madness becomes a metaphor to express that.

Williams: Yes.

Int.: To be taken away.

Williams: Yes. I think it was the only solution for her to go away, to be taken away or to go away. She was not adaptable to the circumstances as they were, that the world had imposed on her. She was a sacrificial victim, you know; she was metaphorical as a sacrificial victim of society.

Int.: There's great wit in her, too.

Williams: Oh quite funny, she's funny.

Int.: She fights with incredible stamina.

Williams: Yes, she fights to the end. She's a tiger, extreme tigers are destroyed, not defeated.

Int.: She had some of the nature of a great poet too.

Williams: Not a great poet; she had had some good speeches but she was eloquent in the way that maybe southern ladies are, you know. I always thought she had her comic side, her little vanities, and her little white lies, but when it came down to the nitty-gritty she wasn't a liar. She told the truth when she had to. But, she was broken on the rock of the world; I find her a sympathetic character but I also find Stanley sympathetic. (laughter)

Int.: Yes, that made a great drama because there was a great conflict there.

Williams: You have to understand both sides.

4. Poetry Referred to in *A Streetcar Named Desire*

Tennessee Williams has written numerous poems and liked to write poetic plays. In *A Streetcar Named Desire* Blanche is shocked when she sees Stella's run-down home. She also expresses her disgust of the surroundings and quotes a line from Edgar Allan Poe's poem "Ulalume" (1847): "Out there I suppose is the *ghoul-haunted woodland of Weir*!" (cf. *Streetcar,* p. 16, ll. 2 f) She thus compares the French Quarter to a horrifying woodland where an evil spirit (ghoul) robs graves and feeds on dead bodies. The last stanza of the poem seems to allude to the reason why Tennessee Williams saw a parallel between Blanche's arrival at Stella's home and the speaker's mysterious arrival in the woodland of Weir:

> Then my heart it grew ashen and sober
> As the leaves that were crisped and sere –
> As the leaves that were withered and sere,
> And I cried – 'It was surely October
> On *this* very night of last year
> That I journeyed – I journeyed down here –
> That I brought a dread burden down here

On this night of all nights in the year,
Ah, what demon has tempted me here?
Well I know, now, this dim lake of Auber –
This misty mid region of Weir –
Well I know, now, this dank tarn of Auber,
This ghoul-haunted woodland of Weir.'
(Edgar Allan Poe, "Ulalume", in: *Selected Writings of Edgar Allan Poe*, p. 83)

When Blanche tells Mitch that the inscription on his silver case is a line from her favourite sonnet by Elizabeth Barrett Browning (1806–1861), Mitch tells her that he got the case from a girl who died. Tennessee Williams employs a quotation from a poem which refers to love and death. It seems to refer to Mitch's and Blanche's loss of their lovers and their longing for love which they are unable to realize.

Elizabeth Barrett Browning: Sonnet from the Portuguese XLIII

How do I love thee? Let me count the ways.
I love thee to the depth and breadth and height
My soul can reach, when feeling out of sight
For the ends of Being and ideal Grace.

I love thee to the level of every day's
Most quiet need, by sun and candlelight.
I love thee freely, as men strive for Right;
I love thee purely, as they turn from Praise.

I love thee with the passion put to use
In my old griefs, and with my childhood's faith.
I love thee with a love I seemed to lose
With my lost saints, – I love thee with the breath,
Smiles, tears, of all my life! – and, if God choose,
I shall but love thee better after death.

5. Literary Criticism

Tennessee Williams' works have been analyzed and commented on by numerous literary critics, who also quoted several statements of the playwright. The following selection of some critics' views of *A Streetcar Named Desire* and the dramatist's work in general could be useful to understand Tennessee Williams' work. You could also refer to them in connection with the impulses and tasks in Chapter VII and consider to what extent you agree or disagree to the critics.

5.1 Francis Donahue: *The Dramatic World of Tennessee Williams*, New York: Frederick Ungar, 1964.

"To the casual reader or playgoer, Williams' plays are unpleasant. They present the seamy side of American life, and they do not have happy endings. They plumb the depths of problems such as homosexuality, symbolic cannibalism, alcoholism, and lurid behavior. And Williams' general view of life is pessimistic, morbid, and tragic." (pp. 202 f)

Donahue also quotes Tennessee Williams:

"A writer's view of the world is always affected by his own state of being. I am an anxious troubled person. I cannot write about anything I don't feel. [...] I am a deeply disturbed person and I write about disturbed people." (pp. 212 f)

"For me, the dominating premise has been the need for understanding and tenderness and fortitude among individuals trapped by circumstances." (p. 212)

"I can't handle people in routine situations. I must find characters to correspond to my own tensions. If these people are excessively melodramatic, well, a play must concentrate the events of a lifetime in the short span of a three-act play. Of necessity, these events must be more violent than life." (p. 212)

"My chief aim in playwriting is the creation of character. I always had a deep feeling for the mystery in life, and essentially my plays have been an effort to explore the beauty and meaning in the confusion of living." (p. 212)

Referring to *A Streetcar Named Desire* Francis Donahue distinguishes the following themes (cf. pp. 225 ff) and character types (cf. p. 229):

Themes:

1. The conflict between reality and illusion

[...] an individual who carries within his or her being an image of the ideal world, is forced to live in a world of a very different nature. [...] He [Williams] seems to regard the delusions of his characters as pathetic defenses against the shipwreck of their lives. Yet he is modern enough to see that the world of illusion in which his hero or heroine would prefer to live is often as corrupt as the physical mundane world in which they are confined.

Blanche DuBois, for example, has keyed her life and thinking to a Southern way of life composed of beautiful clothes, fine manners, and established aristocratic values. But at the time of the play(1947) this way of life has disappeared. The Southern belle is surrounded by bowling alleys, buses, a jazz piano, and a squalid tenement existence. The inner world in which she would prefer to live contrasts sharply with the world in which she has to live.

2. The destruction of the sensitive and romantic by the insensitive and unromantic.

3. The destructiveness of time/time is slipping away

4. The search for beauty in an ugly world

5. The conflict between the spirit and flesh

6. The consequences of nonconformity, e. g. homosexuality

Character types:

1. Blanche, the fragile, pathetic Southern woman who is unable to cope with her problem of living

2. Stanley, the male animal, brutal and coarse

3. Stella, the naive, healthy, yea – sugar [AE address of a person] of the universe

4. Mitch, the average American who conforms to the dictates of his society

5.2 Esther Merle Jackson: *The Broken World of Tennessee Williams*, Madison (Wisc.): The University of Wisconsin Press, 1965.

Esther Merle Jackson underlines that Tennessee Williams' main theme is "the exposure of human suffering" (p. x) and that, like Hart Crane, he is concerned with the reality of a 'broken world'." (p. 26) She believes that "the dramatist describes the human condition as a state of metaphysical loneliness." (p. 29) "Williams's construction of his anti-heroic protagonist, his 'negative saint', is based on a radical perception of new dangers of mankind [...]. In *A Streetcar Named Desire* the playwright cautions the spectator against societal regression, against the capitulation of humanity to the laws of the jungle." (p. 72) "Williams exposes Blanche's progressive fragmentation." (p. 81) "Blanche DuBois reveals her inner nature by playing out her conflicted roles: schoolteacher, Southern belle, poet, sister, savior, and prostitute." (p. 84)
"For like these writers [Ibsen, Strindberg, Beckett, Pinter, etc.] he [Williams] purposes to shock the spectator into recognition of his moral condition by exposing both his public and private sins." (p. 131)

5.3 Peggy W. Prenshaw: "The Paradoxical Southern World of Tennessee Williams." In: Jac Tharpe (ed.): *Tennessee Williams: A Tribute*, Jackson: University Press of Mississippi, 1977, pp. 5–29.

Peggy W. Prenshaw states that the playwright's "characters and themes are built upon paradox" and "embody the opposition within themselves. [...] Williams' world view is his ambivalence of belief [...]. He can neither disbelieve nor believe that life has significance" (p. 9).

6. Reviews

6.1 A drama critic's review

As Tennessee Williams' plays have often provoked the audience and the critics because of their "unpleasant" themes, the reviews are negative or positive. The reviews of his first two successful plays *The Glass Menagerie* and *A Streetcar Named Desire* were predominantly positive, whereas the plays written after 1962 were too "experimental" or shocking to be appreciated by the critics and the audience.
The day after he had read the following review by Brooks Atkinson in *The New York Times*, Tennessee Williams wrote a letter to him in which he expressed his gratefulness (cf. his letter of December 15, 1947 in Chapter IV).

Brooks Atkinson, "First Night at the Theatre" (*The New York Times*, December 14, 1947); quoted from: Richard F. Leavitt (ed.): *The World of Tennessee Williams*, New York: G. P. Putnam, 1978, p. 78:

> Tennessee Williams has brought us a superb drama, "A Streetcar Named Desire", which was acted at the Ethel Barrymore last evening. And Jessica Tandy gives a superb performance as rueful heroine whose misery Mr. Williams is tenderly recording. This must be one of the most perfect marriages of acting and playwriting. For the acting and playwriting are perfectly blended in a limpid performance, and it is impossible to tell where Miss Tandy begins to give form and warmth to the mood Mr. Williams has created.
>
> Like "The Glass Menagerie," the new play is a quietly woven study of intangibles. But to this observer it shows deeper insight and represents a great step forward toward clarity. And it reveals Mr. Williams as a genuinely poetic playwright whose knowledge of people is honest and thorough and whose sympathy is profoundly human.

"A Streetcar Named Desire" is history of a gently reared Mississippi young woman who invents an artificial world to mask the hideousness of the world she has to inhabit. She comes to live with her sister, who is married to a rough-and-ready mechanic and inhabits two dreary rooms in a squalid neighborhood. Blanche – for that is her name – has delusions of grandeur, talks like an intellectual snob, buoys herself up with gaudy dreams, spends most of her time primping, covers things that are dingy with things that are bright and flees reality.

To her brother-in-law she is an unforgiveable liar. But it is soon apparent to the theatregoer that in Mr. Williams' eyes she is one of the dispossessed whose experience has unfitted her for reality; and although his attitude toward her is merciful, he does not spare her or the playgoer. For the events of "Streetcar" lead to a painful conclusion which he does not try to avoid. Although Blanche cannot face the truth, Mr. Williams does in the most imaginative and perceptive play he has written.

Since he is no literal dramatist and writes in none of the conventional forms, he presents the theatre with many problems. Under Elia Kazan's sensitive but concrete direction, the theatre has solved them admirably. Jo Mielziner has provided a beautifully lighted single setting that lightly sketches the house and the neighborhood. In this shadowy environment the performance is a work of great beauty.

Miss Tandy has a remarkably long part to play. She is hardly ever off the stage, and when she is on stage she is almost constantly talking – chattering, dreaming aloud, wondering, building enchantments out of words. Miss Tandy is a trim, agile actress with a lovely voice and quick intelligence. Her performance is almost incredibly true. For it does seem almost incredible that she could understand such an elusive part so thoroughly and that she can convey it with so many shades and impulses that are accurate, revealing and true.

The rest of the acting is also of very high quality indeed. Marlon Brando as the quick-tempered, scornful, violent mechanic; Karl Malden as a stupid but wondering suitor; Kim Hunter as the patient though troubled sister – all act not only with color and style but with insight.

By the usual Broadway standards, "A Streetcar Named Desire" is too long; not all those words are essential. But Mr. Williams is entitled to his own independence. For he has not forgotten that human beings are the basic subject of art. Out of poetic imagination and ordinary compassion he has spun a poignant and luminous story.

6.2 A book review

You can always depend on the kindness of strangers. A review by Bryn Pearson on *A Streetcar Named Desire* – Tennessee Williams, June 27th, 2002, http://www.ciao.co.uk/A_Streetcar_Named_Desire_Tennessee_Williams_Review

Tennessee Williams' play "A Streetcar named Desire" is a powerful tale of lust, poverty and decay. Being a fairly modern text (1940s) it is very readable and entirely relevant to a modern audience. Sadly for me, I've never seen the whole thing on the stage (I saw an extract once), but to read it is very impressive.

The basic plot: Blanche DuBois, down on her luck is obliged to move in with her sister Stella and Stella's husband Stanley. Blanche is used to living the high life, and is not comfortable 'slumming it' in an apartment where men gather to drink and gamble. The tensions between the three rise, leading to violence and abuse. Blanche is rude, demanding and flirtatious, a combination which gradually enrages Stanley.

One of the difficulties with unravelling the play is that so much of its vital content exists in subtext, and so much of that subtext depends on the unreliable statements made by Blanche. It would appear that Blanche's sexual forays have caused a good deal of the trouble in her life, that she is unable to adapt to having limited financial means, that she is accustomed to trading sex for resources and that she is deeply prejudiced. It's possible to see her as someone who brings her fate on herself, or as a mentally unstable victim who is abused by those around her.

The second difficulty arises from the fact that we see so little of Stella and Stanley without Blanche that it's hard to tell what was normal for them and what is resultant from Blanche's presence. Has Stanley always been a violent man, sexually predatory and ruthlessly dominant, or does this behaviour begin as a response to Blanche's? I suspect the latter, given how Stella relates to her husband, but it is open to interpretation.

The play tackles issues of poverty – both physical and personal. The physical poverty seems to be in many ways the smaller issue. There are also issues of racism – Stanley is of Polish extraction, and Blanche generally has a low opinion of those who are not from Northern European families. Her snobbery, in face of her own poverty and lack of dignity seems hard to justify.

If you read this play, you have to do so carefully, looking closely at what lies behind the lines, what happens in the gaps when no one is speaking, what happens in the episodes you do not see. If you see it on the stage, the work of unravelling and interpreting will largely be done for you; the director having no doubt decided to what extent Blanche is a victim and Stanley an aggressor, and how Stella relates to the two. It is a play that is open to a good deal of interpretation. Certain events are unequivocally true, but the guilt of the parties involved, and the nature of the events can be portrayed in different ways, which makes the play particularly interesting.

This might be the tale of a broken down woman abused and then cast out by the last people in the world she has left to turn to. It might be a play about a woman who tries to use sex for her own ends but who is eventually overcome by her own mental insatiability.

6.3 A film review

Tim Dirks: A Streetcar Named Desire (1951), http://www.filmsite.org/stre.html

A Streetcar Named Desire (1951) is a subversive, steamy film classic that was adapted from Tennessee Williams' 1947 Pulitzer Prize-winning play (his first) of the same name. [Early working titles for the play included *The Moth, Blanche's Chair in the Moon,* and *The Poker Night.*] Playwright Williams adapted his own play for the screen version. This film masterpiece was directed by independent director Elia Kazan (his first piece of work with Williams), a socially-conscious director who insisted that the film be true to the play (that he had also directed on Broadway). However, it was opened up to include places only briefly mentioned or non-existent in the play, such as the bowling alley, the pier of a dance casino, and the machine factory.

The electrifying film tells the feverish story of the pathetic mental and emotional demise of a determined, yet fragile, repressed and delicate Southern lady (Blanche) born to a once-wealthy family of Mississippi planters. Her impoverished, tragic downfall in the squalid, cramped and tawdry French Quarter one-bedroom apartment of her married sister (Stella) and animalistic brother-in-law (Stanley) is at the hands of savage, brutal forces in modern society. In her search for refuge, she finds that her sister lives (approvingly) with drunkenness, violence, lust, and ignorance.

The visceral film, considered controversial, decadent, and "morally repugnant" challenged the regulatory Production Code's censors (and the Legion of Decency) with its bold adult drama and sexual subjects (insanity, rape, domestic violence, homosexuality, sexual obsession, and female promiscuity or nymphomania). Ultimately, it signalled the weakening of Hollywood censorship (and groups such as the Catholic Legion of Decency), although a number of scenes were excised, and new dialogue was written. And the Production Code insisted that Stanley be punished for the rape by the loss of his wife's love at the film's conclusion. In 1993, approximately three to five minutes of the censored scenes (i.e., specific references to Blanche's homosexual – or bisexual young husband, her nymphomania, and Stanley's rape of Blanche) were restored in an 'original director's version' video release.

The three main character roles in the ensemble were played with remarkably triumphant performances, all from various stage play casts. One film poster provided a partial film synopsis and description of characters:

[...]

27 year-old Marlon Brando, in his second screen role (after his first appearance in Fred Zinnemann's *The Men* (1950) and recreating his 1947 Broadway role (it premiered on December 3, 1947), delivered an overpowering, memorable, and raw naturalistic performance (an example of Method acting that he learned at the Actors Studio in New York under Stella Adler) as a sexually-powerful, ani-

malistic, brooding primal brute – Stanley Kowalski, Blanche's brother-in-law [The role was first offered to John Garfield, who rejected it because he felt the role was inferior to the female lead role.]

Unstable, delusional, and vulnerable Southern belle heroine (and former English teacher) Blanche, sensitively portrayed by Vivien Leigh, who recreated her role from the London production of the play (directed by then-husband Laurence Olivier). [Vivien Leigh's character was a logical extension from her Scarlett O'Hara role in *Gone With The Wind* (1939) – a post-Rhett Butler Southern belle exhibiting a patrician facade. She was also beginning to show signs of her own emerging manic-depressive, bipolar illness in playing the part, and only appeared in three more films: *The Deep Blue Sea* (1955), *The Roman Spring of Mrs. Stone* (1961), and *Ship of Fools* (1965). In the Broadway stage production, Jessica Tandy played the role of Blanche. The role was first offered to Olivia de Havilland.

Kim Hunter as Blanche's younger sister Stella (a role she originally played on Broadway) and Stanley's wife – a pivotal role

The controversial film was nominated for a phenomenal twelve nominations and awarded four Oscars (an unprecedented three were in the acting categories): Best Actress for Vivien Leigh (her second Best Actress Oscar), and Best Supporting Awards to Kim Hunter and Karl Malden. This was the *first* time in Academy history that three acting awards were won by a single film [...]. In addition, the Best B/W Art Direction/Set Decoration was given to Richard Day and George James Hopkins for their naturalistically sordid sets. Remarkably, these other eight nominations were defeated:

Tennessee Williams' Best Screenplay nomination

Marlon Brando's Best Actor nomination (his first of four consecutive Best Actor nominations, for *Viva Zapata!* (1952), *Julius Caesar* (1953), and *On The Waterfront* (1954) – the last mentioned film won Brando his first Oscar)

Elia Kazan's Best Director nomination

Harry Stradling's evocative Best B/W Cinematography nomination

Alex North's Best Score nomination for the ultra-sultry, steamy score

Nathan Levinson's Best Sound Recording nomination

Lucinda Ballard's Best B/W Costume Design nomination

and its Best Picture nomination

[...]

7. Tennessee Williams about Censorship

Tennessee Williams, "Letter to Joseph Ignatius Breen, head of the Production Code Administration, October 29, 1950" (*Letters*, Vol. II, pp. 355 f)

In this letter Tennessee Williams tries to explain to Mr. Breen why the censorship of the Production Code Administration is not acceptable to him because it is against essential scenes of the film which convey indispensable truths about the real world.

> Dear Mr. Breen:
>
> Mr. Kazan has just informed me that objections have been raised about the "rape scene" in "Streetcar" and I think perhaps it might be helpful for me to clarify the meaning and importance of this scene. As everybody must have acknowledged by now since it has been pointed out in the press by members of the clergy of all denominations, and not merely in the press but in the pulpit – "Streetcar" is an extremely and peculiarly moral play, in the deepest and truest sense of the term. This fact is so well known that a misunderstanding of it now at this late date would arouse widespread attention and indignation.
>
> The rape of Blanche by Stanley is a pivotal, integral truth in the play, without which the play loses its meaning, which is the ravishment of the tender, the sensitive, the delicate by the savage and brutal forces in modern society. It is a poetic plea for comprehension. I did not beg the issue by making Blanche a totally "good" person, nor Stanley a totally "bad" one. But to those who have made some rational effort to understand the play, it is apparent that Blanche is neither a "dipsomaniac" nor a "nymphomaniac" but a person of intense loneliness, fallibility and a longing which is mostly spiritual for warmth and protection. I did not, of course, disavow what I think is one of the primary things of beauty and depth in human existence, which is the warmth between two people, the so-called "sensuality" in the love-relationship. If nature and God chose this to be the mean of life's continuance on earth, I see no reason to disavow it in creative work. At the same time, I know what taste is and what vulgarity is. I have drawn a very sharp and clear line between the two in all of the plays that I have had presented. I have never made an appeal to anything "low" or "cheap" in my plays and I would rather die than do so. Elia Kazan has directed "Streetcar" both on the stage and the screen, with inspired understanding of its finest values and an absolute regard for taste and propriety. I was fortunately able to see, in "rushes", all but the last three scenes of the picture before I left California. Mr. Kazan has given me a detailed description of the scenes I didn't see as they now exist on the screen. I am really amazed that any question should arise about censorship. Please remember that even in notoriously strict Boston, where the play tried out before Broadway, there was no attack on it by any responsible organ of public opinion, and on the screen the spiritual values of the play have been accentuated much more than they could be on the stage.

The poetically beautiful and touching performance of a great visiting artist, Vivien Leigh, has dominated the picture and given it a stature which surpasses that of the play. "A Streetcar Named Desire" is one of the truly great American films and one of the very few really moral films that have come out of Hollywood. To mutilate it, now, by forcing, or attempting to force, disastrous alterations in the essential truth of it would serve no good end that I can imagine.

Please remember, also, that we have already made great concessions which we felt were dangerous to attitudes which we thought were narrow. In the middle of preparations for a new play, on which I have been working for two years, I came out to Hollywood to re-write certain sequences to suit the demands of your office. No one involved in this screen production has failed in any respect to show you the cooperation, and even deference, that has been called for. But now we are fighting for what we think is the heart of the play, and when we have our backs against the wall – if we are forced into that position – none of us is going to throw in the towel! We will use every legitimate means that any of us has at his or her disposal to protect the things in this film which we think cannot be sacrificed, since we feel that it contains some very important truths about the world we live in.

VII Impulses and Model Tasks

The following impulses and model tasks are based on the knowledge of the preceding chapters and are structured according to the aspects of comprehension, analysis, comment, essay writing and creative writing. But they are not intended to be dealt with one after the other. It is your task to decide which of them are most important to you in order to understand Tennessee Williams and his play *A Streetcar Named Desire*. Moreover, you need not adopt the impulses and tasks exactly as they are suggested here. You may, of course, adapt them more or less to your own ideas and alternatives of approach and analysis. You could also decide to write an essay or term paper on a theme that differs from the topics suggested here.

1. Comprehension

1.1 Tennessee Williams' life and works

Outline the playwright's biography in tabular form and describe the main genres of his works (cf. Chapter I).

Tennessee Williams' life

1911 Born March 26 in Columbus, Mississippi, christened Thomas Lanier Williams. His father Cornelius C. Coffin works for a telephone company and then as a travelling salesman for a shoe company. His mother Edwina Dakin is the daughter of an Episcopal priest in whose rectory Tennessee Williams grows up with his elder sister Rose while his father is away most of the time. He is fond of listening to stories told by their African-American nurse.
1916 Because of diphtheria and Bright's disease he is unable to walk for a year and a half. His mother reads to him from Dickens' novels and Shakespeare's plays.
1918 They move to St. Louis, Missouri where his father gets the job of a manager in a shoe factory, which also means the end of his happy childhood in Mississippi. As he is a sensitive and shy boy, he is intimidated by his father who calls him "Miss Nancy". At school he is ostracized and feels lonely except when he is together with Rose or his beloved grandparents.
1919–1926 His brother Dakin is born in 1919 and tension increases between his parents since his father is a heavy drinker and gambler and his mother

gets hysteric. Rose gets mentally disturbed. Williams writes short stories and poems on a second-hand typewriter and enters University City High School in St. Louis.
1927–1931 He wins his first prizes for an essay and a film review. One of his short stories is published. He travels to Europe with his grandfather and has a mystic experience in Cologne Cathedral. He graduates from high school and attends the University of Missouri at Columbia to study journalism but concentrates more on playwriting.
1932–1943 As he fails ROTC in 1932 his father insists on his leaving the university and to work as a clerk for the shoe company. Though he is exhausted after work he continues writing at night and suffers a collapse in 1935. He moves to Memphis and stays with his grandparents. His first play is produced by an amateur company in Memphis. He reads a lot and is deeply impressed and influenced by Anton Chekhov's works. His favourite poet is Hart Crane because of similar biographical experiences and literary views. His grandfather enables him to study playwriting at the University of Iowa which he leaves in 1938 after taking a degree in English. He continuously writes plays and adopts "Tennessee" as his pen name. He goes to different places in the USA and earns his living by taking various odd jobs. In 1939 he receives a Rockefeller fellowship for young writers. In 1943 he writes screenplays in Hollywood but without success. In the same year his mother allows a brain operation of his beloved sister Rose who was diagnosed schizophrenia in 1937. The operation fails and Tennessee Williams takes good care of Rose throughout his life.
1944–1947 His first great success is the play *The Glass Menagerie*, which is produced in Chicago in 1944 and opens on Broadway in 1945. He receives the New York Drama Critics Circle Award and has suddenly become a famous dramatist. After an eye operation he goes to Mexico and New Orleans in 1946 where he works on the first version of *A Streetcar Named Desire* and finishes the play in Key West, Florida in 1947. It is directed by Elia Kazan and first performed in New Haven and finally on Broadway in December 1947 where it runs for 855 performances. He again wins the Drama Critics Circle Award and also the Pulitzer Prize, the greatest honour an American writer can achieve.
1948–1951 His parents separate and he travels extensively in Europe, the United States and Asia to see various rehearsals and performances of his plays. In Rome he begins to write his short novel *The Roman Spring of Mrs. Stone* which is published in 1950. In the same year the film version of *The Glass Menagerie* is released and in 1951 Elia Kazan directs the film *A Streetcar Named Desire* starring Vivien Leigh, who wins an Academy Reward, and Marlon Brando. For his play *The Rose Tattoo* Williams receives the Tony Award as best play.
1952–1962 In 1952 he is elected to the National Institute of Arts and Letters. Apart from travelling to Europe he also goes to New Orleans and writes

several plays such as *Cat on a Hot Tin Roof* (1955) for which he wins his second Pulitzer Prize. Its cinematic adaptation in 1958 is also a great success. In 1956 the film *Baby Doll* is released based on the screenplay by Tennessee Williams. In 1961 he wins the Drama Critics Circle Award for *The Night of the Iguana*.

1963–1983 He continues writing plays but none of them is really successful. He is depressed by his waning career as a dramatist. Since 1949 he has become dependent on alcohol and drugs. His partner and lover Frank Merlo dies in 1963 which intensifies his depression. He undergoes psychotherapy and is taken to hospital after a physical and mental breakdown in 1969. After his recovery he goes on writing plays, travelling and visiting the revivals of his plays. He is honoured by the Presidential Medal of Freedom and receives several honorary doctorates and other awards. In 1982 he suffers from drug toxicity and dies on 24 February 1983 in the New York hotel Elysée choking to death on a barbiturate-bottle cap.

The genres of his works

About 30 long plays such as *The Glass Menagerie, A Streetcar Named Desire, The Rose Tattoo, Cat on a Hot Tin Roof, The Night of the Iguana*
About 40 short plays
About 100 short stories
Two novels
Screenplays, e. g. *Baby Doll*
A large number of poems
Essays: *Where I Live* (collection)
Autobiography: *Memoirs*, 1975
Ballads, songs, a libretto
Letters, Interviews

1.2 Describe the geographical and historical background to the play.

Tennessee Williams went to New Orleans the first time in 1938 and stayed in the French Quarter, which became the setting of *A Streetcar Named Desire*. The title of the play symbolically refers to the tram line that at his time ran to Desire Street. In his play he also mentions the streetcar that ran to the terminus Cemeteries and to Elysian Fields Street, which foreshadow Blanche's tragic end. He makes use of the L&N train line in some dramatic episodes of his play. In his stage directions and also in the play the dramatist mentions

the Mississippi, the harbour and several other places and buildings such as Lake Pontchartrain and the Cathedral.
He describes the atmosphere of New Orleans, its humid climate and its multicultural and multiracial heritage, which is for instance reflected in the architecture of the Vieux Carré and the peaceful living together of black and white people. His characters also use some Creole, French and Spanish words. The musical heritage of jazz and blues symbolically contributes to the atmosphere and action of the play. He also refers to the city's famous carnival of Mardi Gras, to the nightlife and crime to convey an authentic picture of New Orleans in the 1940s.
The historical background of New Orleans is also alluded to when Stanley mentions the Napoleonic Code, which together with the French Quarter and the French language used by Blanche reminds of the French origin of the city, which formerly was called La Nouvelle-Orléans after the Duke of Orléans. It was the biggest city in Louisiana, a French colony, which was sold by Napoleon to the United States in 1803. Belle Reve reminds of the decline of the old plantation owners whose wealth was based on slavery, which was abolished after the Civil War (1861–65). Whereas the name of DuBois refers to the former French immigrants and their cultural life, Stanley Kowalski represents the new immigrants and the new South of industrialization and materialism, but also of patriotism since Blanche's antagonist is proud of being an American and having survived World War II.

1.3 Write a short summary of *A Streetcar Named Desire* by also taking into consideration the following points:

- Blanche's shock when she arrives at the French Quarter and sees the shabby home of her sister
- Her looking for a drink before Eunice returns with Stella from the bowling alley
- The sisters' happiness when they meet and Blanche's criticism of the apartment
- Blanche's false explanation of the reason of her arrival, her description of her taking care of her dying relatives and her accusation of Stella and the loss of Belle Reve
- Stanley's questions and his first suspicion of Blanche
- Stanley's demand to know the truth about the loss of Belle Reve and to see the documents
- Stella's and Blanche's return from a night out while Stanley and his friends are playing poker
- Blanche meeting Mitch who seems to like her whereas Stanley gets furious and even hits his pregnant wife

- Blanche's and Stella's escape to Eunice, Stella's return to Stanley after his desperate calls for her and Blanche's shock
- Stanley's overhearing Blanche's offensive description of him
- Blanche's wish to marry Mitch and her kissing the young Collector
- Her return from a night out with Mitch, her story about Allan's suicide and Mitch's intention to marry her
- Stanley's information of Stella about Blanche's promiscuous life in Laurel and the true reason of her arrival
- Blanche's dismal birthday supper and her being stood up by Mitch who is informed about her past life by Stanley
- Stanley's birthday present (a bus ticket back to Laurel), which upsets Stella and causes her labour pains and her being taken to the hospital
- Mitch's accusation of Blanche as a liar, her honest description of her despairing situation at Belle Reve and her intimacies with strangers
- Mitch's attempt at raping her and her screaming *Fire!* until he runs off
- Blanche living in an illusionary world and fear of Stanley when he returns from the hospital
- Blanche appearing insane and her fight against Stanley who rapes her
- Stella's deceit of her sister, Blanche's futile attempt at resisting being subdued by the Matron and her trust in the kindness of the Doctor who takes her to a mental hospital
- Stella's refusal of believing Blanche's rape and her intention to continue their family life with the newborn baby
- The poker play goes on as usual

2. Analysis and Interpretation

2.1 Describe and analyze the major characters of the play.

Blanche DuBois

- As she is the protagonist of the play, she is the most important character who appears in each of the eleven scenes and represents the main problem of the play Tennessee Williams deals with, namely the futile attempt at maintaining a way of life that is destroyed by the new society she is not able to adapt to.
- The playwright introduces her in his stage directions as a sensitive and fragile thirty-year-old woman, who is daintily dressed and whose beauty is fading. Her appearance does not fit to the run-down home of her sister and to the poor surroundings of the French Quarter.
- As she takes care of her mortally sick relatives she appears to be compassionate, reliable and faithful. On the other hand she does not help her

sister with the household work but likes to be served by her as if she belonged to a higher social class.

- Her view of the role of women is conventional since she is unable to emancipate but is dependent on men. She wishes to find a man for protection.
- Since she belongs to the class of the aristocratic plantation owners and believes to be rather well-educated as an English teacher, she feels superior to the landlady of the house and also to Stanley who works for a factory. In her opinion Stanley is primitive, uncivilized, even sub-human and has no idea of human progress since the Stone Age, whereas she loves art, poetry and music and describes herself as possessing values such as "beauty of the mind and richness of the spirit and tenderness of the heart" (p. 96, ll. 7 f) which the other characters do not own and are unable to recognize.
- Her ancestors were French Huguenots who immigrated to America. She was brought up at a plantation that was sold piece by piece because her male relatives needed money for their dissolute life. Nevertheless she sticks to the old social and moral values her ancestors violated and thus keeps up a facade of good manners and conventional principles such as man's duty to behave like a gentleman.
- At the age of sixteen she fell in love with a sensitive young man and married him. But when she discovered that he was homosexual, she despised him and did not try to understand or help him. His suicide has become a trauma that frequently haunts her. As she feels guilty of his death she prefers white clothes and takes hot baths as if she wished to appear innocent and to purify herself from a sin. On the other hand she feels anxious and is worried about her situation and tries to quiet her nerves by hot baths.
- Corresponding to her conventional education she attaches great importance on good manners and insists on being treated politely. She also behaves in a kind and polite way as long as she tries to keep up a facade to hide sexual desire, alcoholism and dishonesty. On the other hand she accuses Stella in a direct and rude way and insults Stanley without caring for their feelings.
- Though she is destitute and her sister's home is the only place to go for her, she behaves in a conceited way and possesses lots of fanciful dresses and costume jewellery, which underlines her vanity and the wish to appear attractive.
- She believes that she never lied in her heart but she frequently tells lies for instance to hide her promiscuous life in Laurel and the reason of her dismissal because she wants to be respected. But she tells the truth as soon as she thinks or hopes that Stella or Mitch will understand her and feel compassion. On the one hand she deceives Mitch to marry her but is finally honest to him because it is her last hope that he might change his mind and marry her though it is too late.

- She sometimes behaves in a coquettish way and even flirts with Stanley to appear attractive but is shocked by her sister's sexual relationship to her husband, which she calls "brutal desire". This also applies to her relationship to Mitch because she wants him to desire but also to love and marry her and panics when he tries to rape her.
- She is eloquent and has got a sense of humour and irony but her laughter is sometimes described as hysterical and her irony is rather bitter. When she tells the parrot story at her dismal birthday supper, she is the only person who finds it funny and her humour seems to be a gallows humour.
- She is nervous and easily frightened and afraid of death but believes that desire is life. That is why she behaves promiscuously and deceives herself to find protection with strangers and wishes to find peace when Mitch marries her. When she stresses that she is not guilty of "deliberate cruelty", she deceives herself because she is frequently haunted by her husband's suicide she feels responsible of since she treated him cruelly and did not try to understand and help him.
- Though she is described as a fragile "moth" (p. 12, l. 25) and wishes to be protected, she also behaves courageously when she takes care of her dying relatives, defends her sister against Stanley, tries to defend herself with a broken bottle neck against Stanley's attack and finally wrestles with the Matron.
- She is unwilling to accept reality as it is but seems to live in an imaginary world and also tries to make other people believe in it. That is why she does not tell the truth but tells "what *ought* to be the truth" (p. 89, l. 16). More and more she seems to live in a dream world when she for instance tells that she is asked to accompany Shep Huntleigh on a Caribbean cruise, which is obviously an illusion.
- After being stood up by Mitch and Stanley's cynical birthday present, Mitch's attempt at raping her and being raped by Stanley and deceived by her sister she feels trapped, panics and seems to have become insane.

To sum up, Blanche is presented as a psychologically complex character with various contradictory traits that make it impossible for the other characters such as Stanley and Mitch and even Stella to understand her inconsistent behaviour. Tennessee Williams challenges the readers or the spectators to reflect on her tragic fate and on the problem to what extent her decay is caused by the people and society surrounding her but also by herself. She belongs to the decaying civilization of the old South and is obviously not able or willing to adapt to the new way of Southern life. The playwright, who admires the "raffish charm" (p. 10, ll. 4 f) of the French Quarter, seems to regret that the values of the old South have been replaced by a materialistic new society and feels compassion with Blanche as a last Southern belle.

Stanley Kowalski

- Stanley Kowalski is Blanche's antagonist and represents opposite traits of character to a large extent.
- Whereas Blanche is described as slim and fragile, Stanley is strongly built.
- Contrary to Blanche's "aristocratic" social background Stanley's ancestors are immigrants from Poland. As an auto-parts salesman he belongs to the working class and represents the new industrialized South. He enjoys bowling and playing poker, which can be considered characteristic pass time activities of the working class. Also his use of slang is characteristic of his social position.
- He is proud of being an American patriot and of having survived World War II.
- He is convinced of being the master in his house and macho-like dominates his wife and his friends.
- He is unable to understand Mitch's sorrows for his mother but insults him as a cry-baby.
- He is hot-tempered and gets furious when his domineering role is not respected, especially when he is drunk. On the other hand he can be kind and even cries for his wife after she fled to Eunice.
- His relationship to his wife is mainly based on sexual desire and in the stage directions Tennessee Williams states that "since earliest manhood the center of his life has been pleasure with women" whom he does not really respect since he believes to be the "male bird among hens" (cf. p. 22, l. 25) and calls his wife "baby doll" (p. 44, l. 26) as if she were his plaything.
- He is proud of having pulled Stella down from her social class to his own level (cf. p. 84, ll. 33 f) and he is unable to tolerate Blanche's conventional views and manners and respect her privacy but is impolite, ill-mannered and rude.
- He is realistic and matter-of-fact and unable to understand Blanche's desire for magic, art, poetry and music.
- As he is suspicious of Blanche from the very beginning of the play and believes to be swindled by her he wants to know the truth about the loss of the plantation and her life at Laurel.
- Though he seems to be direct and honest and is unwilling to tolerate Blanche's lies, he pretends not to have heard anything after overhearing Blanche's insults and accusations.
- He seems to be faithful to his wife but rapes Blanche and keeps it a secret.
- As he considers Blanche an intruder who endangers the life he is used to live and also his future family life, he wants to get rid of her without feel-

ing compassion or trying to understand her desperate situation. On the contrary, he rapes her and thus contributes to her mental decline. On the other hand he seems to feel compassion with his wife when she is distressed at the end of the play.

To sum up, though Stanley is presented as an uncivilized and rude character, he loves his wife in the only way he understands love, i.e. sexual desire. Though he beats her when he is drunk and gets furious, he cries for her and seems to be ashamed of his violent behaviour. He is honest to his buddy Mitch and wants to continue his way of life with his wife as it was before Blanche threatened to endanger it as he believes. He finally destroys Blanche by raping her, which he believes is the only way to demonstrate his superiority. Like the other characters he is presented as a character with contradictory traits and not only as the personification of evil who destroys Blanche.

Stella Kowalski

- Stanley's wife has been brought up at Belle Reve and has not totally forgotten the conventional way of life there and what it means to have good manners since she criticizes her husband's bad table manners.
- Nevertheless she has left the plantation and did not take care of her mortally sick relatives but has adapted to her husband's working-class life to a large extent.
- As her relationship to Stanley is mainly based on sexual desire she tolerates his uncouth manners to a certain extent and accepts his domineering role since she knows that he is kind to her again even after having beaten her.
- She is accepts the conventional role of women who are dependent on the money Stanley earns, on being given some pocket money and doing the household work.
- She seems to love her sister and patiently listens to her until she gets upset when Blanche accuses her of having left her alone at Belle Reve to go to bed with her "Polack".
- She is kind to Blanche, who likes to be served by her, and tries to cheer her up.
- She tries to understand Blanche's situation, her deceitful behaviour and vanity and defends her against her husband's accusations. On the other hand she does not accept Blanche's insulting description of her husband as ape-like and does not tolerate her superior attitude towards him.
- She seems to be honest but did not inform her sister about the real state of her home, supports Blanche's attempt at deceiving Mitch into marrying her and arranges to take her to a mental hospital.

- She finally deceives herself when she does not want to believe that her husband raped her sister but intends to continue her family life as if nothing has happened. But her remorse and despair seem to be honest when Blanche leaves her home and she is caressed by Stanley.

To sum up, Stella is also an ambiguous character with contradictory traits. Though she was brought up in a higher social class she adapts to her husband's rather primitive way of life to a large extent since she is driven by sexual desire. Though she loves her sister and tries to help her, she finally deceives her and also herself when she decides to ignore the rape in order to save her family life.

Harold Mitch(ell)

- Mitch is one of the poker players and works for the same factory as Stanley. In World War II he belonged to the same army corps as Stanley, who calls him his buddy.
- He is tall and has a heavy build and keeps himself fit as a member of the New Orleans Athletic Club.
- He takes care of his fatally sick mother and seems to depend on her views and values without being able to decide himself.
- When he sees and meets Blanche the first time he is fascinated by her and easily deceived to believe her.
- As the girl he loved died and he fears to be lonely when his mother dies, too, he is nearly in a similar situation as Blanche who also lost her young husband and feels lonely. That is why he also wishes to marry her.
- At first he appears to be a bit clumsy and shy and is gentle and polite towards Blanche. As he is ashamed of perspiring easily, he is considerate towards her. But when he is informed about her promiscuous past, he becomes impolite, rude and even tries to rape her.
- Though he first tells Blanche that he likes her to be exactly the way she is, he finally shows that he is not able to understand her and accept her as she is. Nevertheless he is depressed and sobs when Blanche is taken to the mental hospital as if his dream of a woman he could love is destroyed.
- He even attacks Stanley because he believes that he is responsible of Blanche's tragic fate since he informed him about her immoral past.

To sum up, Mitch is physically strong but mentally weak. He could have overcome his being mummy's boy and recognize Blanche's honest wish to start a new life with him. Though he seems to be sensitive and compassionate, he ignores her honesty and is unable to understand Blanche's desperate situation and her loneliness though he feels lonely himself.

2.2 Discuss to what extent Blanche or other people are responsible for

- her young husband's suicide,
- the loss of Belle Reve,
- her dismissal as an English teacher,
- her expulsion from Laurel,
- the failure of finding peace and protection with Mitch,
- her insanity,
- her being compelled to leave Stanley's and Stella's home.

2.3 Explain the title of the play by also referring to the tram called Cemeteries and Stella's address.

After the great success of his play *The Glass Menagerie* in 1945 Tennessee Williams began to write a scene he called *The Moth*, which refers to Blanche's fragile character. But he did not continue writing the play until he went to Mexico where he replaced the title by *Blanche's Chair in the Moon*, which alludes to the beginning of Scene Nine when she is alone and sits in an armchair after being stood up by Mitch. Another working title was *The Primary Colors*, which refers to the coloured shirts of the poker players. But then the playwright preferred the title *The Poker Night*, which he kept as a subtitle of Scene Three. Finally, however, when he stayed in the French Quarter in New Orleans, the streetcar with the terminus Desire inspired him to choose the final symbolic title *A Streetcar Named Desire*. He also mentions the streetcar Cemeteries, which alludes to the topic of death and seems to foreshadow Blanche's tragic end symbolically.
Before you explain the title of the play look up a dictionary and consider to what extent the two meanings of the word "desire" apply to the play. When you explain the play's final title, the following aspects could be considered:

- In order to go to her sister's home in Elysian Fields Street, Blanche first takes the tram called Desire, which symbolically hints at her sexual desire, her promiscuous life in Laurel but also to her longing for finding protection at her sister's home. The address of her sister turns out to be a trap and no Paradise where she could find peace (cf. p. 90, l. 24). The tram Cemeteries symbolically foreshadows her tragic end.
- The names of the two trams also introduce the audience into two of the main topics of the play, namely desire and death. To Blanche the opposite of death is desire, which means life (cf. p. 91, l. 20). Throughout the play she is afraid of old age and death and wishes to find protection and peace by making Mitch desire and love her.

- But also the other characters in the play are driven by sexual desire and seem unable to make a difference between desire, passionate love and true love. She accuses her sister of feeling only sexual desire for Stanley, who "sizes women up at a glance, with sexual classifications" (p. 22, ll. 30 f) and finally rapes Blanche.
- Blanche and Mitch seem to be able to love each other at the end of Scene Six because both lost their first love and feel lonely. But Blanche was too young to really love her young husband. After that she was driven by sexual desire to overcome loneliness and her fear of death though she is abused by her "lovers". Mitch is unable to accept Blanche as she is and finally tries to rape her.
- The playwright himself explains the symbolic meaning of the streetcar called Desire in Scene Four when Blanche tells her sister: "What you are talking about is brutal desire – just – Desire! – the name of the rattle-trap street-car that bangs through the Quarter" (p. 52, ll. 33 ff).
- The streetcar is mentioned a second time in the play when Blanche asks Mitch after their night out: "Is that street-car named Desire still grinding along the tracks at this hour?" (p. 64, ll. 17 f) Possibly she again alludes to sexual desire (and love).

2.4 Describe and explain the playwright's stage directions.

Tennessee Williams' stage directions are rather long and detailed. The following aspects could be mentioned:

- They are instructions or suggestions to the stage director and the actors.
- They help the readers to understand the characters and the action.
- Critics can take them into consideration when they write a review of a stage production of the play or a film review.
- The playwright informs about his view of the play referring to the setting, the action, the cast, the costumes, light and sound effects and – most important – how to play the roles.
- He describes the atmosphere and multicultural character of New Orleans and the French Quarter in a poetic way by referring to the mood of the place, the Creole buildings, the multiracial and multicultural character of the city and its permanent Jazz music.
- He informs about the characters' age, size, appearance, social position, behaviour, emotions, etc.
- He describes the narrow apartment which does not allow any privacy and thus contributes to the conflicts.
- The props such as a whisky bottle and Blanche's trunk mentioned by the dramatist are necessary requisites for the characterization of Blanche.

Other props such as the folding bed and the poker table help to understand the action.

- The sound effects such as the blue piano, the polka tune, the shot, the noise of the train, the locomotive and the cathedral bells are mentioned to stress the characters' emotions and state of mind symbolically.
- Also the light effects contribute to the characters' emotions since most of the action takes place in the evening or at night because Blanche is for instance frightened by bright light and tries to hide her true age.
- Several other effects of a modern stage are mentioned to present different actions at the same time such as the crime scene in Scene Ten.
- The combination of several effects stress Blanche's panic and insanity, for instance inhuman voices like cries in the jungle, "shadows and lurid reflections", echoes of "mysterious voices behind the walls, as if reverberated through a canyon of rock" (cf. Scene Ten and Scene Eleven).

2.5 Describe and analyze Tennessee Williams' major themes and motifs.

As Tennessee Williams points out that he can only write about his own experiences and problems which he transmutes into plays, some of his major themes and motifs are also dealt with in *A Streetcar Named Desire*:

- **Desire, love and friendship:** Desire is a fundamental driving force of all the characters in the play and is also called "love" by Stella. Blanche's love of her young husband seems to be a kind of adoration. Mitch obviously loves his sick mother but behaves like mummy's boy. Stanley calls Mitch his buddy but does not really treat him like a friend. Thus the characters seem to be unable to feel true love or friendship based on mutual understanding and tolerance.
- **Loneliness and lack of understanding:** As the characters are obviously not able or willing to understand each other including their weaknesses and flaws they seem to be lonely, which in particular applies to Blanche and Mitch but also to Stella and Stanley since their future family life is based on deceit and self-deceit.
- **Reality versus imagination and illusion:** Whereas Stanley and Mitch insist on being realistic, Blanche prefers magic and seems to live in an illusionary world. But as she tells lies to be accepted and tries to deceive Mitch to marry her, she also seems to be calculating to her advantage until she retreats into her dream world of being rescued when her attempts at deceiving others fail.
- **Disease and death:** Blanche and Mitch are confronted with disease and death since Mitche's mother is mortally sick and Blanche had to take care

of her dying relatives. They have also lost their first lovers and Blanche is haunted by her young husband's suicide throughout the play. She is also terribly frightened by death when the Mexican woman appears and sells flowers for the dead.

- **Violence:** Instead of kindness, compassion and understanding the characters treat each other more or less violently to defend their superior position as they believe, in particular Stanley who finally destroys Blanche.
- **Social roles and moral values:** Social roles are understood in a conventional way. Whereas the men earn the money and behave more or less like machos, women are dependent on them to a great extent and look for protection. Their attempts to emancipate fail or are illusionary, since Blanche is fired because of her immoral behaviour, which is not tolerated by society. Also Mitch is unable to understand Blanche's situation because he is mother's boy. Blanche's plan to leave Stanley together with her sister to establish a shop is unrealistic because she would need the help of her imaginary friend Shep Huntleigh. Several social values such as politeness and good manners and also moral values such as the love of truth, honesty, decency, compassion and help are frequently violated in the play.
- **Religion:** The characters sometimes use the words God, Christ, Jesus or *Madre de Dios* mostly without a religious connotation in exclamations and when they are swearing. But Blanche sincerely expresses her gratefulness to God when Mitch wants to marry her: "Sometimes – there's God – so quickly." (p. 72, l. 11) Finally she describes the cathedral bells as "the only clean thing in the Quarter" (p. 103, ll. 14 f), which underlines her disgust of the way of life there.

2.6 Analyze the form and structure of the play by also referring to the three dramatic units of time, place and action.

The play is a modern tragedy and subdivided into eleven scenes of different length, which are performed without a break. But nevertheless there are certain elements which remind of a classical drama, for instance:

- The playwright seems to stick to the so-called Aristotelian unities to a certain extent. As the action concentrates on Blanche's fate and also the subplots such as the poker scenes are meant to contrast with her behaviour, the unity of action seems to be realized. This also applies to the unity of place because the setting remains the same and all the scenes take place in or outside Stella's and Stanley's apartment. The Aristotelian unity of time, i.e. the action takes place on one day, has rarely been practised in classical plays since it is too artificial. That is why also Tennessee Williams does not realize it.

- But he concentrates the action from Blanche's arrival to her tragic end on about five days, which reminds of the five acts of classical dramas. The first six scenes play on three days early in May and the following four scenes on one day in September. The last scene plays some weeks later as an aftermath of the subsequent scene.
- In the first group of scenes (Scene One to Scene Six) the playwright establishes the major characters, Blanche's desperate situation, her confrontation with Stanley as the antagonist of the play and her meeting Mitch. The traditional motif of marriage at the end of the sixth scene seems to indicate a happy ending.
- But at the beginning of the second group of scenes (Scene Seven to Scene Ten) Blanche's hope to find peace and protection with Mitch begins to turn to despair since she is stood up by him and increasingly driven into panic and insanity, which culminates in the last scene. According to the aspects of a rising and falling action there seems to be a turning point after the sixth scene from tragicomedy to tragedy.
- Critics discuss whether Blanche's rape is the climax of the play but this could mean that the exterior action is considered more important than the interior action since Blanche's mental and emotional helplessness seems to become really evident in the last scene of the play, which at the same time underlines her human dignity though she was abused by men and is deceived by everybody.
- Tennessee Williams seems to lay stress on each scene since all of them are structured according to the principles of controversy, conflict, argument and contrast to arouse and maintain the spectators' attention and interest. He creates suspense in every scene and not only referring to the action of the whole play. For example, Scene One presents Blanche's accusation of her sister and ends with hinting at the confrontation with Stanley and Scene Six seems to lead to a happy ending whereas from Scene Seven on the audience is informed about the truth of Blanche's promiscuous life in Laurel and thus confronted with her increasing despair until her tragic end.

2.7 Describe to what extent Tennessee Williams employs symbols in his play by giving some examples.

As Tennessee Williams believes that "art is made of symbols the way your body is made out of vital tissue" (*Essays*, p. 45) his plays can be described as symbolic plays. Instead of describing people and things in a rather lengthy way, symbols help concentrate the playwright's ideas and express them by one word or symbol only. This also applies to *A Streetcar Named Desire* since already the title of the play has a symbolic meaning:

- The streetcar running to the terminus Desire is a symbol of sexual desire which affects all the major characters in the play. On the other hand it also seems to allude Mitch's and Blanche's wish to love and be loved to overcome their loneliness.
- The name of the second tram symbolically alludes to death and Elysian Fields as Blanche's place of refuge ironically symbolizes the opposite to "Paradise", which she hoped to find first with her sister and then with Mitch when she tells him: "I thanked God for you, because you seemed to be gentle – a cleft in the rock of the world that I could hide in! The poor man's Paradise – is a little peace." (p. 90, ll. 22 ff)
- The Chinese paper lantern Blanche wishes to be put around the naked light bulb symbolizes her wish to hide her fading beauty and true age. It is a means of deceiving Mitch who finally tears it down to see her true face. But the lantern also seems to personify Blanche in a symbolic way because when Stanley tears it from the light bulb and extends it to her, Blanche "cries out as if the lantern was herself." (p. 106, ll. 19 f)
- The hand mirror Blanche uses symbolizes her vanity and the wish to appear attractive, which also applies to her fanciful clothes. When she violently puts the mirror down and the glass cracks, it also seems to symbolize her frustration about her fading beauty.
- Whereas the blue piano is a symbol of the way of life in the French Quarter and its effect on Blanche, the Varsouviana polka and the shot, which frequently remind her of Allan's suicide, are symbols of her guilty conscience.
- In the last two scenes of the play lurid reflections, ghostly shadows, inhuman jungle voices and echoes of mysterious voices symbolize Blanche's mental disturbance and insanity.
- The Mexican woman selling flowers for the dead symbolizes death and even seems to be a personification of death like the allegory of the Grim Reaper in Scene One (cf. p. 21, l. 18).
- The locomotive and the noise of the train seem to stand for violence whereas the cathedral chimes symbolize purity and peace.
- Though most of the symbols refer to Blanche, also the other characters are sometimes described in a symbolic way. When Stanley for instance throws a red-stained package from a butcher's up to Stella, the raw meat seems to symbolize his uncouth character and manners which Blanche describes as the behaviour of a survivor of the Stone Age, who bears "the raw meat home from the kill in the jungle!" (p. 53, l. 35).

Apart from the examples mentioned above you will certainly discover many other symbols that contribute to a better understanding of the play. You could also find out that traditional symbols such as the red colour of love seem to be meant in a different or ambiguous way.

2.8 Tennessee Williams likes to employ imagery. To what extent can *A Streetcar Named Desire* be called a "poetic" play?

As Tennessee Williams wrote many poems he also likes to employ poetic devices in his short stories and plays. You could find many of them in *A Streetcar Named Desire*, which are used to convey a lively and graphic impression. In particular the playwright makes use of images, metaphors and comparisons/similes. Here are some examples:

- In his stage directions at the beginning of the play the dramatist describes the atmosphere of New Orleans and the French Quarter in a poetic way: Unlike other American cities New Orleans has "a raffish charm". "The sky [...] is a peculiarly tender blue, almost a turquoise, which invests the scene with a kind of lyricism and gracefully attenuates the atmosphere of decay."
- Blanche is described in a poetic and metaphorical way since "there is something about her uncertain manner, as well as her white clothes, that suggests a moth." (p. 12, ll. 23 ff)
- She also describes her traumatic experiences in a graphic way and makes use of metaphors, similes and an allegory, e.g.: "I, I, *I* took the blows in my face and my body! All of those deaths! The long parade to the graveyard! Father, mother! Margaret, that dreadful way! [...] had to be burned like rubbish! [...] the Grim Reaper had put up his tent on our doorstep! [...] Belle Reve was his headquarters!" (p. 21, ll. 1 ff)
- Blanche explains her name in a poetic way when she compares it to an orchard: "It [DuBois] means woods and Blanche means white, so the two together mean white woods. Like an orchard in spring!" (p. 41, ll. 20 ff)
- Stanley is metaphorically described as having "the power and pride of a richly feathered male bird among hens" and as a "gaudy seed-bearer" (p. 22, l. 30). He metaphorically calls his wife "baby doll" (p. 44, l. 26) as if she were a plaything.
- As Stella is described as kind and patient, Blanche metaphorically calls her "precious lamb" (p. 15, l. 13) and compares her with "a cherub in choir" (p. 17, ll. 25 f). She ironically compares her with a partridge since she believes that she looks a bit plump whereas she describes herself as a "ruin" because of her fading beauty (cf. p. 17, l. 9). At the beginning of Scene Four Tennessee Williams uses an image to describe Stella's face which expresses her "almost narcotized tranquility that is in the faces of Eastern idols" (p. 47, ll. 6 f).
- The playwright describes Stella's return to Stanley after he hit her in a metaphorical way when "they come together with low, animal moans", which is accompanied by a moaning clarinet. Thus the sound of the musi-

cal instrument is metaphorically presented as human and the human sounds as animal-like.
- The playwright employs the image of quicksand when Blanche tells that she could not rescue her young husband: "He was in the quicksands and clutching at me – but I wasn't holding him out, I was slipping in with him!" (p. 71, ll. 5 ff)
- Stanley frequently uses metaphorical phrases that are commonly known such as "the cat's out of the bag", "to call her on the carpet", "to have her on the hook", to bury the hatchet" and metaphorically calls Blanche "visiting royalty", "canary bird", "Queen of the Nile."
- When Blanche is stood up by Mitch she is worried and confused, which is mirrored in her poetic story about candles where several metaphors, similes and symbols are employed: "I hope candles are going to glow in his [Stella's baby's] life and I hope that his eyes are going to be like candles, like two blue candles lighted in a white cake! [...] His Auntie knows candles aren't safe, that candles burn out in little boys' and girls' eyes, or wind blows them out and after that happens, electric light bulbs go on and you see too plainly" (p. 82, ll. 34 ff).
- In the last scene of the play Blanche describes her death and burial on the sea in a romantic and imaginary way.

To sum up, *A Streetcar named Desire* could be called poetic to a large extent, in particular referring to Blanche's imagination and illusions. But since she is finally destroyed by Stanley, poetry and magic give way to realism. Tennessee Williams, however, seems to nostalgically regret that the Old South has been replaced by the new American way of life. By creating the character of Blanche he seems to keep one of the Southern belles alive in his play.
Finally, when Blanche mentions famous American poets such as Edgar Allan Poe and Walt Whitman, tells that her late husband wrote poems and that one of Elizabeth Barrett Browning's sonnets is her favourite sonnet, calls Mitch her "Rosenkavalier", is waltzing and singing popular ballads, Tennessee Williams underlines Blanche's and his own love of art, poetry and music.

2.9 Analyze and evaluate Blanche's insulting description of Stanley in Scene Four by also referring to the stylistic devices used by the playwright.

Analysis
As Blanche is disgusted at Stanley's manners and his behaviour towards her, she describes him in an extremely offensive and degrading way. The playwright stresses her emotions by various stylistic devices, which he sometimes combines, such as

- Contrast between her and Stella's bringing up and Stanley's ordinary behaviour
- Exaggeration: not only ordinary but "bestial", "ape-like", "sub-human"
- Enumeration: "Eats like one, moves like one, talks like one." – "Such things as art – as poetry and music"
- Repetition for emphasis: "Thousands and thousands of years" – "Don't – don't hang back with the brutes!"
- Simile: "like one of those pictures I've seen"
- Metaphor: "Stanley Kowalski – survivor of the stone age!" – "God's image" – "such kinds of new light have come into the world" – "In this dark march" instead of life
- Image: "Bearing the raw meat home from the kill in the jungle!" – "Night falls and the other apes gather! There in the front of the cave, all grunting like him, and swilling and gnawing and hulking! His poker night! – you call it – this party of apes! Somebody growls – some creature snatches at something – the fight is on!"
- Symbol: "flag" instead of human values
- Exclamation: "God!"
- Appeal: "that we have to make *grow*!"

Evaluation

Stanley overhears Blanche's talk and is deeply hurt though he does not show it. But he protests against being permanently insulted at Blanche's birthday supper when he furiously shouts: "Don't ever talk that way to me! – 'Pig – Polack – disgusting – vulgar – greasy!' – them kind of words have been on your tongue and your sister's too much around here! What do you two think you are? A pair of queens?" (p. 81, ll. 23 ff) But also Stella does not really take Blanche's words seriously since she embraces her husband "with both arms, fiercely, and full in the view of Blanche." (p. 54, ll. 29 f)

Blanche's degrading description of Stanley is one-sided and exaggerated. She is unable to tolerate Stanley's way of life since she judges him from her (former) social position, her conventional bringing-up and her education. She ignores the positive sides of his character. Stanley at first accepts her staying at his home but does not want to be swindled or permanently insulted and degraded by her. He works hard for his family, is happy about his new-born son, enjoys life in his way and is not as simple-minded or primitive as Blanche believes since he easily recognizes her lies and evasions. He is not naive but sceptical and insists on being informed about her and on knowing the truth. When he informs Mitch about Blanche's past, he behaves as a true friend and he loves his wife the way he understands love as based on sexual desire.

Blanche does not realize or is not willing to accept that she has several negative traits of character in common with Stanley such as sexual desire and the violation of moral principles. Because of her conceitedness and illusions she is unable to understand Stanley who is also unable to understand Blanche and her weaknesses. Thus Tennessee Williams underlines his view that people only see and judge others from their own point of view without being able to understand each other.

3. Criticism and Comments

3.1 Comment on some of Blanche's statements such as:

Sorrow makes for sincerity. (p. 41, l. 4)

In some kinds of people some tenderer feelings have had some little beginning! That we have got to make *grow!* (p. 54, ll. 7 ff)

Soft people have got to court the favor of hard ones. (p. 58, ll. 22 f)

A girl alone in the world, has got to keep a firm hold on her emotions or she'll be lost! (p. 65, ll. 26 ff)

I don't tell truth, I tell what *ought* to be truth. (p. 89, l. 16)

The poor man's Paradise – is a little peace. (p. 90, l. 24)

Deliberate cruelty is not forgivable. It is the one unforgivable thing in my opinion and it is the one thing of which I have never, never been guilty. (p. 96, ll. 24 ff)

Those cathedral bells – they're the only clean thing in the Quarter. (p. 103, ll. 14 f)

I have always depended on the kindness of strangers. (p. 107, ll. 35 f)

3.2 Comment on Tennessee Williams' statements about his work and his view of Blanche (cf. Chapter IV,1; VI,1 and VI,2 in this study aid).

3.3 Describe and evaluate Tennessee Williams' view of producing a play for the stage.

Apart from the text IV,2 the following extract from Tennessee Williams' essay *Author and Director: A Delicate Situation* (*Essays*, pp. 93, 97 f) can help you:

Whether he likes it or not, a writer for the stage must face the fact that the making of a play is, finally, a collaborative venture, and plays have rarely achieved a full-scale success without being in some manner raised above their manuscript level by the brilliant gifts of actors, directors, designers, and frequently even the seasoned theatrical instincts of their producers. [...]

And just as a playwright must recognize the value of conceptions outside his own, a director of serious plays must learn to accept the fact that nobody knows a play better than the man who wrote it. The director must know that the playwright has already produced his play on the stage of his own imagination, and just as it is important for a playwright to forget certain vanities in the interest of the total creation of the stage, so must the director. I must observe that certain directors are somewhat too dedicated to the principle that all playwrights must be "corrected." I don't think a director should accept a directorial assignment without feeling that, basically, the author of the play, if it's a serious work by a playwright of ability, has earned and deserves the right to speak out, more or less freely, during the rehearsal and tryout period of the production if this can be done in a way that will not disturb the actors. Yet it sometimes happens that the playwright is made to feel a helpless bystander while his work is being prepared for Broadway. It seems to me that the director is privileged to tell the author to "Shut up!" actually or tacitly, only when it is unmistakably evident that he, the director, is in total artistic command of the situation. Sometimes a director will go immediately from one very challenging and exhausting play production into another, being already committed by contract to do so. Then naturally he can't bring the same vitality to the second that he brought to the first. This becomes evident when the play has been blocked out, and after this blocking, little further progress is being made. The play remains at the stage of its initial blocking. The director may say, and quite honestly feel, that what he is doing is giving the public and critics a play precisely as it was written. However, this is evading the need and obligation that I mentioned first in this article, that a play must nearly always be raised above its manuscript level by the creative gifts and energies of its director, and all others involved in its production.

3.4 Compare Elia Kazan's characterization of the major characters with the playwright's views (cf. Chapters IV–VI) or your own interpretation.

3.5 In the following extract from Williams' essay *The Timeless World of a Play* (*Essays*, pp. 53 f) he describes the reaction of the spectators. Comment on his view by also referring to the behaviour of the major characters in *A Streetcar Named Desire*.

> [...] plays in the tragic tradition offer us a view of certain moral values in violent juxtaposition. Because we do not participate, except as spectators, we can view them clearly, within the limits of our emotional equipment. These people on the stage do not return our looks. We do not have to answer their questions nor make any sign of being in company with them, nor do we have to compete with their virtues nor resist their offenses. All at once, for this reason, we are able to *see* them! Our hearts are wrung by recognition and pity, so that the dusky shell of the auditorium where we are gathered anonymously together is flooded with an almost liquid warmth of unchecked human sympathies, relieved of self-consciousness, allowed to function.
>
> Men pity and love each other more deeply than they permit themselves to know.
>
> So successfully have we disguised from ourselves the intensity of our own feeling, the sensibility of our own hearts, that plays in the tragic tradition have begun to seem untrue. For a couple of hours we may surrender ourselves to a world of fiercely illuminated values in conflict, but when the stage is covered and the auditorium lighted, almost immediately there is a recoil of disbelief.

3.6 Do you think the playwright's view of life as presented in *A Streetcar Named Desire* is totally pessimistic?

3.7 Is *A Streetcar Named Desire* a psychological play, a tragedy or a melodrama?

3.8 Comment on some of the statements of literary critics (cf. Chapter VI,4).

3.9 Comment on one of the reviews (cf. Chapter VI,5).

3.10 Compare the play with its cinematic adaptation by also referring to Chapter V.

3.11 Do you think that the "purified version" of the play or the film should be preferred to the original one and be analyzed at school? Give reasons for your answer.

In order to answer this question, make use of the information given in Chapters I,1 and V.

3.12 To what extent is the German translation *Endstation Sehnsucht* adequate to the American title of the play?

4. Essays, Reviews, Term Papers and Creative Writing

You could write an essay or term paper about one of the following topics and discuss it in your course.

4.1 The American South, in particular Louisiana and New Orleans

Apart from the information given in Chapter I you could make use of reference books and the Internet.

4.2 New Orleans as the cradle of Jazz

You can easily find information on the Internet, e.g.: History of Jazz. Part 1: Elements of Jazz/New Orleans (http://www.jazzitude.com/historleans.htm). There are also several reference books about the history of Jazz.

4.3 On Tennessee Williams' play *The Glass Menagerie*

You could either write about the play, the film or compare the play with its cinematic adaptation. The essay should contain a short summary of the action, the characterization of the major characters and the discussion of the problems of the play.

4.4 Are Tennessee Williams' views of violence, sexual desire and love, the lack of comprehension and compassion also relevant today? Give reasons for your answer.

4.5 To what extent is Blanche a victim of her Southern views and of the society and the circumstances she has to live in?

4.6 In his *Memoirs* (p. 136) Tennessee Williams mentions Thornton Wilder's criticism of Stella's role in the play since "no female who had ever been a lady could possibly marry a vulgarian such as Stanley." Do you think that this is justified? Give reasons for your answer by referring to the play.

4.7 On Tennessee Williams' play *A Streetcar Named Desire* – a book review

After reading the play you could first give a short summary, describe the characters and then deal with some of the major problems and give reasons for your views. Though the review is based on your opinion about the play, you could also make use of the information given in this study aid (cf. Chapters I–III and VI).

4.8 On a stage performance of *A Streetcar Named Desire* – a review

Possibly you saw a stage production of the play in English or German. You could write a review and also compare it with the drama critic's review in Chapter VI.

4.9 Elia Kazan's adaptation of *A Streetcar Named Desire* – a film review

After seeing and analyzing the film you could also make use of the information given in this study aid (cf. Chapters V and VI). Terms for film analysis you can for instance find in *Brewer's Cinema* (1955), in Arijon, *Grammar of the Film Language* (1991) or on the Internet.
Moreover, you could inform about the film director and the major actors, Elia Kazan, Vivien Leigh and Marlon Brando. Information could be downloaded from the Internet (e.g. http://www.kirjasto.sci.fi/kazan.htm, http://en.wikipedia.org/wiki/Vivien_Leigh, http://en.wikipedia.org/wiki/Marlon_Brando).

You could also refer to Williams' view of Vivien Leigh as presented in the following extract from his essay *Five Fiery Ladies* (cf. *Essays*, pp. 127 f) and compare the playwright's impression of the actress with your impression when you see the cinematic adaptation of the play:

> Vivien Leigh is not only the officially appointed first lady of the London theater, but several other things of equal or greater importance: an actress of great talent which has steadily grown through meeting the challenge of many classic roles, Greek, Shakespeare, Restoration, and Shaw, while still appearing so masterfully in such American films as *Gone With The Wind* and my own *Streetcar*. At present she is appearing in a film based on my novel, *The Roman Spring of Mrs. Stone,* a part she accepted with no reluctance despite its being an aging actress, retired from the stage and infatuated with a young adventurer more interested in mirrors than anything except money.
>
> Her beauty, Vivien's, is as delicately flamboyant as an orchid. When she takes the stage, she commands it as if she first arrived there suspended from the bill of a stork.
>
> Vivien, above all else, is incomparably graceful, she moves like a marvelous dancer, on or off stage, and she has an instinct for doing and saying just the one right thing to put you at ease even when you know you are making a fool of yourself. All of these wonderful gifts she has given with no apparent regard for her personal vulnerability: in other words she is not only a stunning actress but a lady with the most important part of that intricate composition, which is kindness of heart.

You could also mention Williams' first impression of Marlon Brando, who visited him in Key West (cf. *Conversations*, p. 337):

> Then, before he was famous, Brando was a gentle, lovely guy, a man of extraordinary beauty when I first met him. He was very natural and helpful. He repaired the plumbing that had gone on the whack, and he repaired the lights that had gone off. And then he just sat calmly down and began to read. After five minutes, Margo Jones, who was staying with us, said, "Oh, this is the greatest reading I've ever heard, even in *Texas*!" And that's how he was cast in *Streetcar*.

You could structure your review as follows:

1. Introductory statement on the genre and the theme of the film
2. Reasons for the pros and cons referring to questions such as:
   To what extent does the action correspond to the play?
   Is the setting well chosen?
   How do costumes, props, etc. support the action?
   Is the camera work adequate to the presentation of the setting, the characters, the major problems, etc.?
   What is the effect of the soundtrack, lighting and costumes?
   What is the quality of the cast?
3. Final statement about the quality of the film (reasons for or against it)

4.10 After having read the play and/or seen the film, you could imagine to write an interview with Tennessee Williams in which you ask questions that – in your opinion – the playwright did not answer to your full satisfaction. Try to give the answers also based on the knowledge you gained by this study aid.

4.11 Before Tennessee Williams decided to call his play *A Streetcar Named Desire*, the titles of his first drafts were *The Moth, The Poker Night, The Primary Colors, Blanche's Chair in the Moon* and *Paper Lantern.*

- Task (re-creation of text): Discuss the various titles and point out to what part of the play each title mainly refers and to what extent it would affect the interpretation of the play if it were the final title.
- You could also suggest a different title such as *Belle Reve, Elysian Fields, The Broken Mirror, Blanche's Dream, Longing for Peace*, etc. and explain why and to what extent it could also apply to the play.

4.12 Tennessee Williams first thought that the ending of *A Streetcar Named Desire* was too harsh. He therefore experimented with different endings, for instance with a near promise of marriage since Mitch forgives Blanche. Another ending the playwright thought of was that Blanche secretly desires Stanley, earns his respect and goes away somewhere "in search of life."

Task (re-creation of text): Considering the different endings of the play and the film you could write your own ending of the play and give reasons why it could also be adequate.

Bibliography

Browning, Elizabeth Barrett: Sonnets to the Portuguese. In: The Poetical Works of Elizabeth Barrett Browning in Six Volumes. London: Smith, Elder, & Co., 1889–90. [Sonnet XLIII in Vol. IV, p. 77.]

Cole, Toby / Chinoy, Helen Krich: Directors on Directing. A Source Book of the Modern Theater. Revised Edition. Ninth Printing. Indianapolis / New York: Bobbs-Merrill, 1963.

Debussher, Gilbert: Creative Rewriting: European and American Influences on the Dramas of Tennessee Williams. In: Roudané, Matthew C. (ed.), pp. 167–188.

Dirks, Tim: A Streetcar Named Desire (1951): http://www.filmsite.org/stre.html

Donahue, Francis: The Dramatic World of Tennessee Williams. New York: Frederick Ungar, 1964.

Fergusson, Rosalind: The Penguin Dictionary of Proverbs. Harmondsworth: Penguin, 1983.

Hayman, Ronald: Tennessee Williams. Everyone Else Is an Audience. New Haven / London: Yale University Press, 1993.

Hornby, A. S.: Oxford Advanced Learner's Dictionary of Current English. Seventh Edition. Oxford: Oxford University Press, 2005.

Jackson, Esther Merle: The Broken World of Tennessee Williams. Madison (Wisconsin): The University of Wisconsin Press, 1965.

Jauslin, Christian: Tennessee Williams. Velber: Friedrich, 1969.

Kazan, Elia: *Notebook for "A Streetcar Named Desire"*. In: Cole, Toby / Chinoy, Helen Krich, pp. 364–379.

Leavitt, Richard F. (ed.): The World of Tennessee Williams. New York: Putnam, 1978.

Leverich, Lyle: Tom. The Unknown Tennessee Williams, New York / London: W. W. Norton, 1995.

Londré, Felicia Hardison: A Streetcar Running Fifty Years. In: Roudané, Matthew C. (ed.), pp. 45–66.

Palmer, R. Barton: Hollywood in Crisis: Tennessee Williams and the Evolution of the Adult Film. In: Roudané, Matthew C. (ed.), pp. 204–231.

Pearson, Bryn: A Review on *A Streetcar Named Desire* – Tennessee Williams, June 27th, 2002: http://www.ciao.co.uk/A_Streetcar_Named_Desire_Tennessee_Williams_Review

Poe, Edgar Allan: Selected Writings. Ed. by David Galloway. Harmondsworth: Penguin, 1967.

Potter, Simeon: Our Language, Harmondsworth: Penguin, 1968.

Prenshaw, Peggy W.: The Paradoxical Southern World of Tennessee Williams. In: Tarpe, Jac (ed.): Tennessee Williams: A Tribute. Jackson: University Press of Mississippi, 1977, pp. 5–29.

Roberts, James L.: *The Glass Menagerie* and *A Streetcar Named Desire*. Lincoln (Nebraska): Cliff Notes, 1999.

Rogers, Ingrid: Tennessee Williams: A Moralist's Answer to the Perils of Life. Frankfurt am Main / Bern: Lang, 1976 (Europäische Hochschulschriften, Reihe XIV, Bd. 44).

Roudané, Matthew C. (ed.): The Cambridge Companion to Tennessee Williams. Cambridge: Cambridge University Press, 1997.

Sambrook, Hana: Tennessee Williams: *A Streetcar Named Desire*, London: York Press, 2003 (York Notes).

SparkNotes: A Streetcar Named Desire. Tennessee Williams: http://www.sparknotes.com/lit/stretcar.html

Spoto, Donald: The Kindness of Strangers. The Life of Tennessee Williams. Boston: Da Capo Press, 1997.

Tharpe, Jac (ed.): Tennessee Williams. A Tribute. Jackson: University Press of Mississippi, 1977.

Tischler, Nancy M.: Tennessee Williams: Rebellious Puritan. New York: The Citadel Press, 1961. [Quotations taken from Hana Sambrook: *A Streetcar Named Desire*. London: York Press, 2003.]

Twentieth Century Interpretations of *A Streetcar Named Desire*. Ed. by Jordan Yale Miller. Englewood Cliffs (New Jersey): Prentice-Hall, 1972.

Wentworth, Harold / Flexner, Stuart Berg: The Pocket Dictionary of American Slang, New York: Simon & Schuster, 1968.

Williams, Dakin / Mead, Shepherd: Tennessee Williams. An Intimate Biography. New York: Arbor House, 1983.

Williams, Tennessee: The Major Plays. Ed. by Benjamin Nelson. Englewood Cliffs (New Jersey). Prentice-Hall, 1985.

– Plays 1937–1955. Ed. by Mel Gussow and Kenneth Holdich. New York: The Library of America, 2000.

– A Streetcar Named Desire. New York: New Directions, 2004.

– A Streetcar Named Desire, with an introduction and annotations by Horst Mühlmann. Stuttgart: Ernst Klett, 2008.

– A Streetcar Named Desire. Ed. and annotated by Helmut Wolf. Frankfurt am Main / Berlin / München: Diesterweg o.J. (Diesterwegs Neusprachliche Bibliothek).

– A Streetcar Named Desire. Hrsg. von Herbert Geisen. Stuttgart: Reclam, 1988 (Fremdsprachentexte).

– A Streetcar Named Desire. An Elia Kazan Production. Produced by Charles K. Feldman. Warner Bros. Entertainment Inc. Distributed by Warner Home Video, 2006 (DVD).

- Conversations with Tennessee Williams. Ed. by Albert J. Devlin. Jackson/ London: University of Mississippi, 1997.
- Memoirs. New York: Doubleday & Company, 1975.
- On a Streetcar Named Success. In: Williams, Tennessee: Where I Live. Selected Essays. Ed. by Christine R. Day and Bob Woods. New York: New Directions, 1978, pp. 15–22.
- The Selected Letters. Ed. by Albert J. Devlin / co-ed. by Nancy M. Tischler. Vol. II. 1945–1957. London: Oberon Books, 2006.
- Where I Live. Selected Essays. Ed. by Christine R. Day and Bob Woods. New York: New Directions, 1978.

Internet addresses and search engines

http://en.wikipedia.org/wiki/A_Streetcar_Named-Desire
http://en.wikipedia.org/wiki/Louisiana
http://en.wikipedia.org/wiki/Louisville_and_Nashville_Railroad
http://en.wikipedia.org/wiki/Marlon_Brando
http://en.wikipedia.org/wiki/New_orleans
http://en.wikipedia.org/wiki/Tennessee_Williams
http://en.wikipedia.org/wiki/Vivien_Leigh
www.google.de/search?hl=de&q=Tennessee+Williams
www.imdb.com – Internet Movie Database
www.kirjasto.sci.fi/kazan – Elia Kazan
www.mrqe.com – Movie review Query Engine
www.film.com – Reviews, news, interviews
www.jazzitude.com – History of Jazz
www.oscars.org – (Official Academy Awards site)
www.stlouiswalkoffame.org
www.tennesseewilliams.net/index.php?topic

Acknowledgements

S. 9: Picture-Alliance, Frankfurt/M./Langenstrassen – S. 17: Getty Images, München/Hulton Deutsch – S. 58: AKG, Berlin – S. 106: ullstein bild, Berlin

Der Verlag hat sich bemüht, alle Inhaber von Urheberrechten an Texten und Abbildungen zu diesem Werk ausfindig zu machen. Sollte dies in irgendeinem Fall nicht korrekt geschehen sein, bieten wir an, nach Anforderung rechtmäßige Ansprüche abzugelten.